Endorsements

I have read scores of books and articles about blood covenant from E.W. Kenyon to the present. Daniel Donaldson's intricate details are amazing, instructive, inspiring, and impactful for living an abundant life in blood covenant with Jesus Christ. Theologically and practically, this book is a must-read for every Christian who desires to know Christ more intimately."

-Dr. Larry Keefauver, Bestselling Author and International Teacher

Daniel J. Donaldson has done an extensive look into the Blood Covenant and has masterfully brought its impact and importance into everyday life! From the illustrations to the historical context of the Blood Covenant, Daniel has made this a must read for anyone who wishes to go deeper in their faith and understanding of the covenant that God has made with us.

-J. Michael Ruggerio, Lead Pastor Crossroads Worship Center
Sewell, New Jersey

THE
MYSTERY OF THE
BLOOD
COVENANTS

THE MYSTERY OF THE BLOOD COVENANTS

Unveiling the Secret of Enjoying Covenant

Grace, Faith, and Favor

DANIEL J. DONALDSON

XULON PRESS

Xulon Press
2301 Lucien Way #415
Maitland, FL 32751
407.339.4217
www.xulonpress.com

Paperback ISBN-13: 978-1-6322-1135-4
Ebook ISBN-13: 978-1-6322-1136-1

Dedication

To our Lord Jesus, and my wife Lindy.
Your faith in me and love for me
Have always been the secrets to my every success.

Table of Contents

INTRODUCTION

Another Life-Changing Book, Really?

✠

I believe all books have the potential to change the lives of their readers for the better or for the worse. More than fifty years ago, I read a book in the Second Grade at Center Street Elementary School in El Segundo, California. The book told the stories of the heroic inventors Henry Ford, Thomas Edison, and The Wright Brothers. Burned into my memory is most of its content. My mind still sees some of its pages bearing large, easy to read Century Schoolbook font and simple illustrations.

The writer's intent may have been to make its content interesting enough to keep a young reader's attention while learning the fundamentals of reading. Nonetheless, the stories still had a profound life-changing effect on me. I credit that book with being used of God to inspire many of my life's most rewarding pursuits, lifelong passions, and successful professional career as an inventor.

I pray that this book will have a significant and impactful life-changing effect on your life and relationships. What you are reading and implementing through the truths of the blood covenant will change your life.

How can I be so sure?

- Because knowing and cutting the blood covenant with God is absolutely vital to correctly understanding the whole Bible.

- Because in discovering these truths myself, I have experienced a closer walk with Christ and a more Christlike way to love others as I love myself.

✠

**For many Christians, the Bible remains a riddle,
wrapped in a mystery, inside an enigma.[1]
Is that true for you?**

✠

One reason is that those outside the church, with their own agenda, have worked very hard to try to kick "blood covenant" to the curb as superstitious nonsense and irrelevant fiction. Worse yet, religious organizations have supplanted its truth with the traditions of men. As Jesus explains, "Making the word of God of none effect through your tradition, which ye have delivered..."[2] The Strong's Concordance translates "of none effect" as "to render void, deprive of force and authority."

Over time, even the true significance of the names of the two primary sections or collections of books in the Bible has been all but lost. Names intended to help clarify their collective topics and importance, now tend to shroud it more. If you were to ask someone why the Old Testament and New Testament bear those names, they likely would say something like this. "The older books of the Bible contain stories about God and mankind that take place before Jesus was born. The newer books start with the story of the birth of Jesus, and tell about His life

---

[1] [1]Attributed to Winston Churchill.

[2] Mark 7:13 (KJV)

and death, and the history of the early church." This explanation, you will see, is more than a quart shy of a full gallon.

May I ask you...

Is there any one simple and understandable way to show how the modern thought that would dismiss the relevance and veracity of the Scriptures is itself irrelevant fiction and unmasked nonsense?

Can this same simple and understandable truth be universally applied to reveal what the accurately taught truth of God is, and what are the traditions of men masquerading as truth?

Is it even possible for one overarching theme to embrace, put in proper context, and yield a right understanding of all books of the Bible?

Are some parts or whole passages of the Bible difficult for you to understand? With what you have in place now as the foundation for your believing, are you experiencing the abundant joy, complete inner peace, enviable fortune, and spiritual prosperity that Jesus said should be the defining attributes of your life? If not, you are not alone.

Is there a simple way to take almost every Scripture that ever made us scratch our heads where they do not itch and reveal their true and proper interpretation? Yes, there is. It is to have revealed to us the breadth, length, depth, and height of the mystery of the Blood Covenant Truth.

Could not knowing the mystery of the Blood Covenant
be what is keeping you from inheriting all that is yours
in Christ?

Well, consider this. Not perceiving the mystery of the Blood Covenant is irrefutably what caused most of those who had been following Jesus, and actually heard the words of Jesus, to reject Him! One of the most important things Jesus said to His Hebrew Covenant kinsmen nearing the end of His public ministry was:

And Jesus said to them, I assure you, most solemnly I tell
you, you cannot have any life in you unless you eat the flesh
of the Son of Man and drink his blood."[3]

Jesus was speaking to those who ironically prided themselves on being well-informed covenant heirs, descendants by birth of Abraham. They were marked in their flesh with the covenant sign of circumcision. Yet, the Jews did not understand this passage that can only be understood in light of the covenant-making significance of the terms Jesus used. Without that understanding, the hearers, who steadfastly held to the Covenant Law of not drinking the blood of animals, presumed Him to be advocating cannibalism and began to fall away in droves.

If their hearts had been open to discern instead of hardened to spurn, they could have been among the first to perceive and receive the Covenant-based Promises of forgiveness, righteousness, peace, joy, love, healing, and restoration. The good news for them, the Apostle Paul later explained, is that one day Abraham's descendants by natural birth will see and accept Jesus as their Covenant Lord and King.[4]

What is wonderful is that it is possible for their loss to be our gain. But here is the rub, and that is the reason I believe Father God laid it

---

[3] John 6:53 (AMPC)

[4] Romans 11:26

upon my heart to write this book. One can read the New Testament accounts of what Jesus said and did, just as His first audience, without really understanding its message that is *purposely* hidden in plain sight. A read through the Bible cover to cover, void of covenant understanding, can leave you even more clueless than Jesus' unhearing hearers.

I am absolutely confident that if you read this book with an open heart and mind, your next read through any book of the Bible will be a mind-blowing experience. Passages will open to you as quickly as a flower going from bud to full bloom when filmed in elapsed time. The Holy Spirit will be able to reveal truths that you did not even know could be known and you can be set free in ways you did not think it possible to be set free. This is my hope, prayer, and confident expectation for you.

-1-

How Living the Blood
Covenant Life Changed Mine

✠

Let me share another reason why I am wildly confident that reading this book will change your life for the better. It is because the later part of my life is a forty-year testimony to the revelation of the mystery of the blood covenant doing for me, what I am saying it will do for you.

Most personal testimonies are divided into two parts by the teller. They have a B.C. era, defined as their life Before Christ, and an A.C. era defined as After Christ became their Savior. I never had the era defined above as a B.C. life. I was born again at my mother's knee cognizant of what I was doing, at the ripe old age of five. I attended churches, some requiring a coat and tie of the truly devout, others where even the pastor taught in business casual attire, all my life.

I was going to church like clockwork, but maybe this will show how even when my age was measured in single digits, I somehow sensed that what I got from attending church was not bad, but it also was not the whole story. The smaller you are, the larger the old Thomas Kinkade-esc steepled and stained-glass windowed *House of God* looks. I was in awe of its majesty, but there were drawbacks. Hard pews, little sounds echo, and little Danny has to stand quietly at attention for "The Prayer."

1

That five minutes of prayer intoned with Elizabethan English "thees and thous" droned on prior to us children being dismissed to go downstairs to our Sunday School Class. This proved conclusively Albert Einstein's theory of time. Things really do take far longer or far less time depending on how much you are enjoying the event. For me, it was about as much fun as having a tooth pulled through the ear canal.

Whew...downstairs in the basement was a different world. There we had fun and colorful decorations all over the walls and chairs my size. At Christmas, there was what they called a nativity set, and there was also a guy in a red suit thereabouts. We were enthralled by Bible Stories told with the help of cut out characters adhering as if by magic to a flannel covered board on an easel. (Next gens or later, Google "Flannelgraph.")

One thing confused me enough to finally interrogate my Sunday School teacher about it. I had been in every corner of the upstairs and downstairs that did not have a locked door.

"Ma'am?"

"Yes, Danny?"

"Is this *really* God's House?"

"Yes, Danny, it is."

"Well, I just wondered. Where does He go on Sundays, when we come over to use it?"

She did not have an answer, but I still liked going there to hear the stories.

Perhaps those stories contributed to why I never fell away from my conservative Christian upbringing even as a teenager, despite raging hormones. I remained a virgin until marriage, never smoked, and contrary to some public figures, neither lit up nor inhaled any marijuana. This was all the more remarkable for a kid growing up in Southern California in the '60s and '70s. This was the epicenter of where Hippies preached a message of Sex, Drugs, and Rock and Roll. Please understand, I am not boasting in this as there were times I wanted to do anything and everything I was not allowed to do. I credit the fear of God, the love of my parents, and the grace of God lavished on me unawares for making it out of my adolescence with my testimony such as it was, intact.

My point is, that as much as possible, I was a Bible-believing, sold-out Christian through all my school years. This culminated in graduation from an academically tough and highly acclaimed, conservative Christian College, magna cum laude. With a major in English and minor in Biblical Studies, I was hoping to make a living writing books the *New York Times* bestselling author Eric Metaxas describes as "genuinely entertaining and solidly biblical." Some heartfelt dreams planted by the Lord might have to take a back seat for a few decades as mine has. But that does not mean they were kicked out of the car, right?

Meanwhile, I did shelve those thoughts of being an author for a time. Immediately after graduation, life happened. I had married the love of my life during my senior year of college. I scraped through my pre-grad years on an academic scholarship and an on-campus job cleaning the dorm halls and toilets of kids who did not, for $1.35 per hour. I had to borrow the $200 dollars for my bride's wedding ring from my father. I drove a ten-year-old VW Beetle that lacked seat belts and heat. Suffice to say, I was not a spoiled rich kid partying his way through college.

My first paying job after graduation was as a bank teller. Back then, we tellers hand-sorted and filed the canceled checks of our account holders into Pendaflex folders at the branch. I could not help peeking at the amount on the surprisingly modest salary checks of Mr. Brown, the Branch Manager. I realized at that point, that just because we were employed at a bank, this did not mean its money would be our money. I then was given the opportunity to manage a Radio Shack store, then oversee a large number of them, and then open their first Computer Stores in Los Angeles. This required sixty-hour workweeks and another twenty hours a week commuting, depending on traffic.

This then, for many years, was my B.C. life, which I define as "Before Covenant." I was working myself literally to death, both that of my physical and spiritual lives, as well as putting a horrible strain on my marriage. On the surface, it looked as if the little church we attended was rightly dividing the Word in their statement of faith, but more often they were wrongly dividing the congregation with church splits over the traditions of men.

I frankly was not enjoying my Christin life, but I feared more the prospect of leaving the church doors unrepentant, getting run over by a truck that same day, and spending eternity separated from God in hell. I was taught and believed Christians must suffer affliction, spurn riches, keep all the 10 Commandments without fail, and confess and then ask forgiveness again for each one I broke anyway, just before taking communion. To do otherwise would be to risk bringing more damnation on my soul.

No worries, if I ever got out of line, the Holy Spirit was there, at arms-length, to convict me of my sins and drag me back to the straight and narrow path. While this life may be hard, I was assured that on some mission field in Africa someone was having a much harder time serving God than I was (and they were). I was afraid to try to get any closer to God lest He ask me to also serve on a mission field, go through what I thought He did to Job, or make demands of me tantamount to the unthinkable like He asked Abraham to do. If I was not careful, Jesus would make me sick so that He could teach me a lesson. It makes no sense to me now, but at the time, it was exactly what I believed.

I sincerely believed that if my faith was strong enough and I did not walk away from Him altogether, Jesus would give me the strength to endure to the end. Then after I died, all the blessings, riches, treasure, health, joy, peace, and life abundant the Bible spoke of would be mine in Heaven. I never stopped to ask why the rather large and very beautiful home I desired to have for my young family, but would never be able to afford, was wrong to even desire to have while here, but that colossal mansions are perfectly okay to have in heaven.

The Blood Covenant

Then it happened. One day I dropped in quickly to say hi to my mom and she said, "I have something I want you to listen to, a cassette I got from a preacher on the radio." I asked what it was about, and she handed it to me. All it said on the label was *The Blood Covenant*. I was very skeptical, but I loved my mom and did not want her to get caught up in some unscriptural appeal from a charismatic (in that day this was to me a derisive term synonymous with pew jumping Holy Roller) preacher. I smiled and took it with me, fully intending to rip its message to shreds in minutes with the sum total of my scholastic and biblical acumen.

There was a problem with that. As I began to listen, the southern twang was a bit strange to my ears, but every word of it made total sense to my heart. He was telling me what I did not know that I did not know. I was familiar with many of the verses, but never took a class on the subject of the Blood Covenant in all my biblical studies. Still wondering if some of the scriptures were misinterpreted or taken out of context, I jotted down and then read each quoted verse, and then the whole chapter of scripture surrounding that verse. It got worse (I mean, of course, better for me, worse for my B.C. self's pride).

Furthermore, the Scofield notes in the King James Version could not come to my rescue. Nor did the Harper Study Bible, nor the Strong's Exhaustive Concordance. Does Romans really say that? Uprooting trees was not just a figure of speech? Healing miracles can still happen today? We can increase our churches exponentially instead of dividing them? We can be free from crushing debt in the midst of a recession? Does Hebrews really say that? Does Galatians really say that? Even Genesis, does it really say that?

Fortunately, I did one thing right years earlier. I made and kept the vow to always allow the Bible to be the final authority on the Bible. If the science teacher said one thing, and the Bible said something else, I believed the Bible. If a Bible teacher said one thing, and the Bible said something different, I believed the Bible. If my own long-held beliefs said one thing, and the Bible said something different, I would have to change my beliefs to line up with the Bible. The more I studied the more I could see it was true that understanding the Blood Covenant was the key to having an abundant life and a better relationship with Father God, Jesus, and the Holy Spirit on *this* side of the grave.

I went to my old Youth Group leader I had known for years and told him the good news of what I discovered. He recoiled and refused to accept it. "But look," I said, "See what it says here in Ephesians?" The response was visceral, "I know it looks like it is saying that, but we do not believe that in our church, so it must not be true."

I kept on studying what I came to love and loving what I came to know. I have shared some of what my B.C. (Before Covenant) life looked like. Now if you permit, I will share a glimpse at the transformation that became my A.C. (After Covenant) life.

I discovered that Father God was *not* the one leading me into temptation, He is the one who is ready, willing, and more than able to deliver me *from* evil. God revealed my deepest desires and dreams were from Him. All desires and dreams could be unleashed into my life with His blessings. I mentioned earlier that I can credit one of the earliest books I ever read with being used of God to inspire many of my life-long passions, pursuits, and successful professional career. A.C., this became a reality.

As to lifelong passions, one would be a love of the automobile inspired by Henry Ford: I have owned an authentic Ford Model A Roadster, a Ford Thunderbird, and a Ford Escape. Also: Chevrolet S-10, Volkswagen Beetle, Chrysler Le Baron, Chrysler Sebring Convertible, Classic 1972 Plymouth Satellite Sebring Plus, Toyota Cressida Hatchback and Sedan, Subaru Hatchback, Honda Accord, Mercedes CLK 430, Hyundai Sonata, Cadillac Allante, Buick Riviera, Buick Regal, Dodge Caravan, Lexus LS 430, and Genesis G80. Though I did not own them, I have driven a Mercedes Gull Wing, Lamborghini, and Tesla on test courses. To round it out, I attended a Winston Cup NASCAR Race trackside, with Garage access and a Hot Pits Pass.

As to life-long pursuits, I have a Wright Brothers inspired inordinate love of flying. I have flown in an early WW1 Era Biplane, co-piloted a WW2 T-6 Aerial Dogfight Trainer, blimps large and small, an ultralight aircraft, hang glider, and parasailed. I have soared in a Glider, floated in Hot Air Balloons, and jumped out of a perfectly good airplane to Skydive.

I have copiloted Cessnas for lessons, but never got a license (still on the Bucket List). As a commercial passenger, I have marked off my Bucket List the goal of flying over one million miles with Delta Airlines. I copiloted the larger blimp only a few feet above the Hudson River Bridges to see Lady Liberty eye to eye, back when they allowed it. I buzzed the Colorado River below the Rim of the Grand Canyon in a helicopter, like Luke Skywalker attacking the Death Star, before that was also outlawed. Finally, to honor the memory of my heroes of flight, the Favor of God made it possible for me to attend the reenactment of the Wright Brothers' flight at the First Flight Centennial at Kitty Hawk in 2003.

A final evidence of their enduring inspiration I submit is a prized possession hanging on my Dan Cave wall. I was able to obtain a piece of the original fabric covering their famous Model EX *Vin Fiz Flyer* from the Smithsonian Museum of Flight for helping fund their restoration work.

Last but not least, is my homage to the influence of Thomas A. Edison. My childhood dream was not to be a sports star, Hollywood star, or astronaut exploring the stars. The story of Thomas Edison inspired me to become an inventor of electronic devices that truly make a difference in how things are done.

There is actually some DNA also influencing me. I learned the rudiments of electronic circuitry from my electronic technician wizard of a father Parish Freeman Donaldson. I got something far better than just book learning while I helped him for years in our family-owned radio and TV repair business. He shared with me an inventor's knack for making things work regardless of expert opinions to the contrary. As part of a literally secret life, my father invented the first underwater missile guidance system motors and helped install the first radar early warning defense systems across the country.

This is not an autobiography, so let me cut to the chase. I seized the opportunity to become a personal computer guru when the entire systems had less memory in them than a PC mouse does today. I grew with the industry, and in 1999, invented the first digital microfilm product that allowed users to do microfilm roll research by looking at the live image of the film on a PC screen. When I came up with the idea, there were almost no computers in libraries, and the microfilm was viewed in a darkened area by reflecting it with a mirror onto a pane of glass. My discovery literally changed the way we look at microfilm. Today, the only way you can view more than a million rolls of microfilm housed at thousands of libraries all over the world, and at America's Library of Congress, is to use one of my ST Imaging ViewScan systems.

✠

None of this is my own doing, I am simply going along for the ride, going where God-given Covenant grace, Covenant faith, and Covenant favor take me.

✠

In spiritual pursuits, I have twice, literally, uprooted overgrown trees that were damaging my property with prayer and by speaking to them.[5] I regularly pray for the seemingly impossible and see the manifestation. God Himself through the Holy Spirit took up residence inside this old house, not inside a church building, so I could employ the gifts of the Spirit to help others. I have helped build three local churches. When I first attended a church in Las Vegas, we met in a store-front rental space. Before I moved away, we purchased property that today houses a worship center, a Christian school, and has a televised national outreach.

Our San Diego church grew from meeting in a Middle School auditorium in Rancho Bernardo to be located in a gorgeous modern structure that looks like an early California mission, complete with tree-lined plaza and fountain. In New Jersey, miraculous events the pastor and I were led to pursue helped take us from a single story forty-year-old 10,000 square

---

[5] After a season of prayer, on two separate occasions, micro climate storms uprooted each tree, with no damage to property, other trees, or other plants.

foot cement slab cinderblock building, to a four-story 60,000 square foot cathedral and campus.

As to healings, there have been many, but topping the list is being miraculously and completely healed twenty years ago from a virulent form of advanced kidney cancer (Renal Cell Carcinoma), without Chemo.

✠

One thing that understanding Blood Covenant has produced that I value above all others is a transformed prayer life and intimate relationship with the Father, Son, and Holy Spirit.

✠

B.C. Daniel could not be cajoled into praying for more than five minutes on sporadic days. Now, A.C. Daniel prays, praises, simulates dancing, thanks, and communes with the Lord for a minimum of two hours every day; a source of pleasure rather than pain.

Summarizing, to know the mystery of the Blood Covenant is to come to know more than ever, and better than ever, the breadth, length, depth, and height of the love of The Covenant Maker. I can truly say my Blood Covenant infused life is what Jesus promised it would be in Matthew 5:8.

> *Blessed (happy, enviably fortunate, and spiritually prosperous—possessing the happiness produced by the experience of God's favor and especially conditioned by the revelation of His grace, regardless of their outward conditions....* (AMPC)

Key Points: Review and Reflect

Take a moment and review the key points and questions asked in this chapter. Reflect on how they can change your life as they did mine.

> *As you reflect on the scriptures and insights I share in this book, will you strive to allow the Bible to be the final authority on the Bible instead of man-made traditions and beliefs?*

> *Is your life infused with what Jesus promised it would be in Matthew 5:8?*

> *If Father God, being no respecter of persons can do what He has for me through teaching me about the Blood Covenant, what might He do for you?*

Pray and ask the Holy Spirit to reveal truths that you did not even know could be known and set you free in ways you did not think it possible to be set free.

Begin to keep a journal of what the Holy Spirit reveals to you as you open your heart and mind to receive God's truths through this study of the Blood Covenants.

-2-

How did the Mystery of Making Blood Covenants Form Ancient Civilizations, World Religions, Wedding Cakes, and Christianity?

Small tribal communities, developing regional groups, nations, states, and whole ancient civilizations that defined the borders of countries are all built upon the same fundamental elements of communal living. There are agreements to do things together under a commonly held and understood set of terms and conditions. There are agreements on how to conduct commerce, agreements that define political governance, agreements as to who or what to worship and obey religiously, and agreements that define matrimony.

Ancient Civilizations

The more important agreements that formed the basis for ancient civilizations would, in some cases, predate written history and writing itself. Certainly before, and even after society developed written communication, there had to be a way to memorialize agreements, especially the more important ones. I find it very interesting that modern language still includes in its deal-making terminology some elements of how more important agreements were made long ago.

"How did that important deal you were working on for the property turn out?"

"Great! I was able to *cut* a deal with the owner that we both liked."

When you "cut a deal" today, you usually mark the paper with your signatures. The ancients would "literally cut" their agreements. For agreements that dealt with something less than life and death issues, ancients would make a verbal agreement in the presence of witnesses, and would also cut symbols into the surface of a stone, tree, animal, doorpost, or later a clay cuneiform tablet, or later still put a mark on paper.

Really important agreements throughout ancient history, recent history, and even nowadays will include putting a mark on one's flesh to attest to a sacred agreement. I remember a company pool party I attended years ago. Since we were all in bathing attire, I could not help noticing a young black man's scar. My coworker then explained to me why there was a three-finger-wide keloid scar in the shape of the Greek letter Omega on his chest, just above his heart. Having it was a matter of pride to him because it represented the lifelong commitment he made to his Omega Psi Phi college fraternity brothers. This took place over thirty-five years ago. I did not work closely with the young man and I do not remember his name, but I never forgot seeing the mark of his covenant.

The Cut

The Hebrew word used in the Old Testament, תיְרִב, *Beriyth*, ties together the act of making a cut with the act of making a sacred agreement. Its meaning is literally "to cut a covenant." The cut made in the human flesh would not be life-threatening. It was made so that a small amount of blood from the cut could be mixed in one way or another with that of the other covenant maker. Often, a cut would also be made in the flesh of an animal that would ensure that the blood of the animal was shed and death would occur. It was understood that the life of the animal represented and stood in the place of the lives they would be willing to give for one another.

The Covenant

The modern English word covenant is derived from the Latin *convenire* meaning "to come together, unite, and come into agreement."[6] When I purchased my home, a condition of sale was that I sign an agreement affirming that I would come together, unite, and agree on codes of conduct for as long as I live there, with the other homeowners in my community. I must abide by their CC&Rs: Covenants, Conditions, and Restrictions.

The Blood

The Bible tells us, "For the life of the flesh is in the blood."[7] It has been proven in practice and instilled in the heart of man from the beginning that having our blood in us sustains life and spilling our blood equates to death. It is hardly a stretch to then see how the blood of man and beast can easily come to represent their life, their very being.

What do you suppose would be a way to describe the significance of an agreement that would set it apart from the trivial, temporal, or less important agreements?

How might you set forth that the agreement's participants are entering into a lifelong agreement as dear as life itself? It would be, it has always been, to cut a blood covenant.

---

6 https://biblehub.com/greek/3762.htm

7 Leviticus 17:11 (KJV)

World Religions

When out of fear a group concedes power over their lives (erroneously) to things created such as weather patterns, sun, moon, stars, mythological beings, or doctrines of demonically fallen angels, they tend to hold to these self-imposed detrimental agreements religiously. Strictly enforced codes of conduct and rites of initiation seal the deal of becoming a member of religious communities. Though leaders of some man-made religions maintain power by including rituals that are hidden to outsiders, we know that virtually all of them include initiates participating in a blood oath ceremony. Hence, the elements of making a blood covenant are found in the formation and practice of World Religions.

The proper practice of Christianity should not be confused with the practice of World Religions. It is not surprising that some organizations borrowed ideas and symbols from the Bible to form their religious knock-offs. No one makes a counterfeit $3.00 bill. Some just twist or borrow what they will from Scripture. Others have rewritten and handed out their own edited version of a "bible" to give their cult a feigned credibility. As we continue through this study, we will see how Christianity does also have a blood covenant at its heart. Yet, the terms and conditions, as well as the nature of its participants, and what they did to put it in place, set it apart from all others.

Wedding Cakes

When two ruling families want to consolidate political power, they can arrange a marriage. Since the power of the countries was so often vested literally in the bloodline of its rulers, mixing the blood of the two families through the progeny of the marriage made a way for the two families to become one alliance.

Even if the couple getting married will only be ruling their own household, a marriage affects the families of both of them for life. A Mother-in-Law and a Father-in-Law get their new names by reason of children not born to them now becoming the same as their own children by reason of law—marriage covenant law. Most often the union leads also to future generations of children in whom the flesh's encoded attributes, DNA, of both mother and father are found.

For these reasons, there was and indeed should be a ceremony performed to be witnessed by friends and family of the bride and groom that will be affected by the union. This is a life-changing event, for better or for worse. In that ceremony, the marriage couple would, before these witnesses, make and exchange solemn blood covenant Oaths of Wedding. The definition of the word wedding is; *to bind by close or lasting ties, attach firmly together.* During the wedding ceremony, there would be a single cup of wine from which both would drink. There would also be a cake or cakes of bread made for the occasion. A cake would be cut, and the two new partners in life would eat from the same piece of cake. Later, all of the attendees would eat of the cake. Now you can see how making covenants is why we are still to this day making wedding cakes for wedding ceremonies.

Christianity

The thread of blood covenant promises begins in the first chapters of Genesis and runs through the life and times of every book of the Old Testament and New Testament, right up to the last chapters of Revelation.

I believe God placed the concept of making solemn and sacred blood covenant promises in us from the very beginning. Covenant making was a vital part of His plan to provide redemption for us from the breaking of that first covenant between God and Man by Adam and Eve.

✠

Mankind may not always keep their covenant promises, but God always does.

✠

15

There are reasons why the significance and implications of making blood covenant promises is a veiled mystery throughout the Old Testament and the Gospel books in the New Testament. One reason the words and actions of Bible characters are often puzzling to us today is that we have been cut off from a basic understanding of blood covenants.

Why did Samson's strength leave him when he cut his hair?

Why was teenaged David comfortable bringing a rock to a sword fight with a nine or more-foot-tall seasoned warrior?

Why did Isaac not retract the blessing he pronounced over Jacob when he found out that he had been tricked by Jacob into giving it to him by impersonating his brother?

Why did David treat the grandson of the King he deposed as if that child was his own, with no fear of retaliation or vying for his throne?

As we make our way through the Mystery of the Blood Covenant, the reasons for these curious actions and more will be revealed. Much of what baffles us about what Bible characters did is because we do not know what adhering to covenants makes covenant makers do.

Almost everyone portrayed in these books knew what it meant to be bound by a blood covenant relationship, even if they were heathens. How is it then, that almost all of them misunderstood what God was really doing by way of the blood covenant promises He made? Even the New Testament Gospel books, Matthew, Mark, Luke, and John, show people missing the true covenantal meaning behind what Jesus said and did. They complained that He spoke in riddles. That is because He did. The covenant promise being fulfilled in the life of Jesus was a priceless treasure being purposely hidden in plain sight. We can easily err just as they did, if we, as did they, and attempt to understand and apply the sayings of Jesus spoken about as the new wineskin (covenant) while using an old wineskin (covenant) mentality. This often resulted in rock-throwing.

Jesus was on a secret mission to become the greatest Covenant Maker of all time. Yet, it had to remain veiled until He completed His assignment. Why? Here is the solution to that riddle.

*No, we speak of the mysterious and hidden wisdom of God, which He destined for our glory before time began. **None of the rulers of this age understood it. For if they had, they would not have crucified the Lord of glory.** Rather, as it is written: "No eye has seen, no ear has heard, no heart has imagined, what God has prepared for those who love Him."*[8]

The crucifixion was not an accident, a tragedy, or a mistake. It was the final mysterious act of God cloaking the Light in the darkness, thereby keeping His covenant promise to sacrifice His own son. The plan had to remain veiled until the instant of Jesus' death. At that moment, the literal veil in the old wineskin's Temple, which had separated man from God, was rent in two.

*"When Jesus had cried out again in a loud voice, He yielded up His spirit. At that moment the **veil** of the temple was torn in two from top to bottom. The earth quaked and the rocks were split."* (Matthew 27:50-51 Berean Study Bible)

Father God had hidden the mystery of salvation by this blood covenant sacrifice in His post-expulsion promise to Adam and Eve. While passing sentence on their tempter, God said: "And I will put enmity (open hostility) between you (Satan) and the woman, and between your seed (offspring) and her Seed; He shall [fatally] bruise your head, and you shall [only] bruise His heel."[9]

Jesus is also referred to in Scripture as the last Adam.[10] He is the one referred to in the prophetic verses above as "her Seed." Jesus, though

---

[8]   Berean Study Bible emphasis added by the author

[9]   Genesis 3:15 (Amplified Bible)

[10] Thus it is written, the first man **Adam** became a living being (an individual personality); the last **Adam** (Christ) became a life-giving Spirit [restoring the dead to life]. (AMPC)

fully God, would empty Himself of divine privilege to be a man, born of woman. Yet, He would not succumb, as the first Adam and all mankind had done, to the Serpent's temptations to disobey God. This would enable Him, while in the process of having His flesh injured for the first time on the cross, to use that very act to crush the head of our enemy. This kept promise from "in the beginning" formed the basis for a restored relationship in the end. His blood covenant sacrifice made it possible to have a new blood covenant relationship with Father God. This new basis for a relationship with Father God is what formed and is only found in Christianity.

Evidence of Blood Covenants Everywhere

There is irrefutable evidence of making blood covenants for one reason or another, and some of the variances in how they are done in tribes, regions, nations, states, countries, and religions all over the world. This is seen in H. Clay Trumbull's exhaustive study of the subject, *The Blood Covenant*. The work had its start by the author studying to present findings on the subject in lectures conducted in 1885. The book that grew out of those lectures has become the definitive work on the history of the practices for more than one hundred years. Its seventh printing of the second edition is still on the virtual shelves of Amazon Books.

Dr. Trumbull details innumerable variances in the ceremonies that are sometimes gruesome (licking one another's blood from cuts) and sometimes bizarre (wiping a few drops of blood from each covenant maker onto tobacco that was formed into a cigarette, lit, and both inhaled). More common was cutting the two covenant makers, placing a drop of their blood in a cup of wine, and then both drink from the same cup. The ceremonies differed, yet with virtually all having in common certain fundamental points of agreement as to what it means to enter into or cut a blood covenant. Diverse peoples doing this include Semitic, Hamitic, Japhetic,

Asian, African, European, American, Islands of the Seas, Caucasian, Mongolian, Ethiopian, Malay, and many more.[11]

Also important is the fact that there are proofs of the simultaneous independent existence of the rites in these diverse places and cultures that had no know interaction, yet with common ground in what it means.

✠

This points to the inescapable conclusion of a common inherent heartfelt origin of the practice common at the earliest stages of human communal living.

✠

Blood Covenants in the Bible

We have seen how the four general categories of covenant agreements we have been looking at, i.e. friend-based commerce, political, religious, and marital, define and form the basis for communal living. All of these can be seen in the Bible. In some cases, it might even go by unnoticed that the Bible story is depicting covenant life, practices, or ceremonies.

Two men could become blood brothers strictly for purposes of commerce or enduring friendship, pooling their resources. Two neighboring clans could come together to cut a blood covenant with each other to share the water of a well or grazing land, rather than to wage a war spilling the blood of one another for control of the vital resources. A king whose story is being told in scripture can be seen making or breaking a covenant promise to the subjects of his realm. A marriage is in progress as we see blood covenant elements materialize at a wedding ceremony in Capernaum. In addition to men and women covenanting with one another, the Bible shows us multiple covenants God made with mankind and creation.

---

[11] H. Clay Trumbull, *The Blood Covenant.*

Bible scholars have given names to some of the covenants God made with men and women, usually associating them with the name of their human participants.

Noahic Covenant: Noah and creation are promised protection from the flood.

Abrahamic Covenant: Abraham is promised that he will father the Seed spoken of in Genesis 3:15.

Mosaic Covenant: Moses brokers the deal requested by the Hebrew Children to substitute a covenant with Laws they could try to keep in lieu of a face to face relationship with God. (They chose poorly.)

Davidic Covenant: David is promised the throne of Israel and that his Seed would always rule after him.

New Covenant: Jesus cuts this blood covenant with God on behalf of all men. All former covenants and promises are fulfilled and replaced by a New and Better Covenant.

These are the big five, arranged in chronological order. Some equally important covenant relationships, in terms of helping reveal the mystery of the blood covenant, are not listed in the traditional treatment of the subject in Bible study handouts or Wikipedia. These other covenant relationships include the God's covenant promises to Adam and Eve, Isaac, and Jacob, David's Covenant with Jonathan, and covenants Hebrew clans cut with neighbors. There are also glimpses of covenants underlying and impacting the lives of heathen kings, Israel's enemies, the disciples, and the followers of Jesus before the New Covenant was ratified.

I will only touch on some of these blood covenant relationships in this book, by no means exhausting the subject. My purpose in writing goes beyond documenting the clear importance and centrality of blood covenants throughout the Bible. My mission is to pull away the veil, revealing how the blood covenant that defines our relationship with Father God works. Knowing this will greatly multiply your ability to understand the Bible as a whole and its Gospel message of a new and better covenant relationship.

The Gospel, which means the Good News, is not limited to the news that Jesus died on a cross and rose again to save us from our sins. Some of the largest Protestant Church organizations to grow out of the Reformation still preach and teach, that while we know Jesus did die on a cross, thousands of other people did also, and their deaths did nothing for us, which of course is true. They say emphatically that no man knows, and no man can hope to know exactly *why* Jesus dying on a cross saves us. They say you just have to have faith and believe it does anyway, without knowing why, that it is just a mystery.

The good news is that they are mistaken on that point. I know this sounds bold and boastful, but it is not. What for some remains a five-hundred-year-old mystery is irrefutably and wonderfully solved. I thank Father God for gracing me with what I am sharing with you regarding the covenant promises being kept on that day when Jesus was crucified. We will see exactly how and why the specific manner of His death was a required part of the Old Covenant promise He was fulfilling, and the New Covenant promise He was making. Grace, faith, and favor will increase as we learn why Jesus died in the way that He did, when He did, where He did, and how He did, on a cross, and then being raised from the dead.

✠

The Good News is that as a result of what Jesus did that day, a New Covenant authored by Father God and signed with the blood of Jesus, is now ours for the taking.

✠

Key Points: Review and Reflect

Take a moment and review the key points and questions asked in this chapter. Reflect on how they can change your life as they did mine.

Forgiveness of sins is only one of many benefits. Here are a few more to ponder as we dig into how and why cutting covenants works.

> *Bless (affectionately, gratefully praise) the Lord, O my soul, and forget not [one of] all His benefits—*
>
> *Who forgives [every one of] all my iniquities,*
>
> *Who heals [each one of] all my diseases,*
>
> *Who redeems my life from the pit and corruption,*
>
> *Who beautifies, dignifies, and crowns me with loving-kindness and tender mercy;*
>
> *Who satisfies my mouth [my necessity and desire at my personal age and situation] with good so that my youth, renewed, is like the eagle's [strong, overcoming, soaring]!*
>
> *The Lord executes righteousness and justice [not for me only, but] for all who are oppressed.* (Psalm 103:2-6 AMPC)

Fact: We tend to believe what we say. I modified these verses from the original text only to personalize it, replacing the words "you" and "your" with the words "me" and "my."

Pray and start every day of the next full spin around the sun saying these verses out loud.

22

Journal how praying this prayer and opening your mind and heart to begin to understand how the covenant promises Jesus fulfilled increases the grace, faith, and favor in your life.

-3-

Making Blood Covenants:

✠

How do they work?
How do you make them?
What's with the pile of rocks here?

W e have seen that people could have very different reasons for cutting a covenant. Two men could become blood brothers strictly for the purposes of commerce, friendship, and pooling their resources. Two neighboring clans could come together to cut a blood covenant to share the water of a well or grazing lands rather than going to wage war. Both benefit from spilling a little blood during a ceremony rather than a lot of one another's blood for control of the vital resources. We see that a wedding ceremony is actually a blood covenant-making event. Father God built man for fellowship with one another and with Himself. That is why He instituted the practice of making blood covenants and practiced doing so with mankind.

I find it amazing that while the participants and the motivation to come together may differ, very similar ceremonial practices are followed and symbolize the same cardinal aspects—ground rules they are to abide by—when being covenanted together.

Let's look now at some common ground rules that define what covenants are, how covenants work, and what will take place during covenant-making ceremonies. What is being done may be obvious, but what it means and why we do it may be a bit of a mystery. In this chapter, we will reveal the great symbolic importance of what is done when covenants are made. This will reverberate throughout the remainder of the book, in the end, unveiling the final and greatest mysteries surrounding the greatest blood covenant ever made. These elements of the ceremony are all part of what the covenanting partners are promising to do for each other when making a blood covenant.

What does it mean to be in a blood covenant relationship?

The majority of all covenants found in the Bible are made between two people or groups of people who may not be equal in size, strength, wealth, or possessions, but both bring something to the new relationship. The only covenants we are concerned with in this treatise are those that are consensual. This is because the ones of greatest importance to us are those made between God and men, and those are always consensual.

The party offering to be in a covenant relationship and the one agreeing to accept that offer must be doing so of their own free will. They agree to treat one another as equals in and to the extent of what is being covenanted to be shared, to the full extent that their respective resources permit. Both parties benefit, not just the lesser or the greater. The lesser obviously benefits by now being able to claim the blessings that accompany a covenant relationship with the greater. What the lesser brings to the relationship enables the greater to become greater still. Covenanting partners are saying, "For better or worse, for richer or poorer, all I have is yours, and all you have is mine."

✠

If all I have is yours and all you have is mine, how are blood covenant partners prevented from taking advantage of one another?

✠

The mystery of asking your covenant partner to do a favor for you.

If all you have is mine, and all I have is yours, how are covenant partners prevented from taking advantage of one another by what they ask for from one another? Is this or is it not a rather important question to get an answer to? What I am about to share is a potentially life-changing covenant truth. In fact, this is one of the **most important mysteries** I unveil in this book. We will see it in action many times in future chapters, but I want to introduce it and lay the foundation here. This is not just an example of how blood covenants work. The principle of how blood covenant favors work is the foundation of love-based covenant-making.

✠

There is a difference between covenant gifting and asking for a favor and its importance cannot be overstated.

✠

Covenant gifts begin to be exchanged while a covenant is being made and at any future time as the givers so choose. They are given without repentance. That means the gifts are given without the possibility of a later change of mind. Scripture tells us this is true concerning the gifts that are given by Father God to us.[12] That means He will not change His mind and ask you to return them. The Amplified Bible explains, "For God's gifts and His call are irrevocable. [He never withdraws them when once they are given, and He does not change His mind about those to whom He gives His grace or to whom He sends His call.]"

There may be conditions that need to be met, but they are known and merely need to be met to receive the gift. One such condition might be that you may be required to simply ask in good faith for gifts that have already been made available to you as part of your covenant agreement.

---

[12] Romans 11:29, "For the gifts and calling of God are without repentance." (KJV)

You are not taking advantage of your covenant partner when you ask for a gift to be given to you that was already expressly offered to you. You are in fact dishonoring him or her if you refuse to accept a gift that is freely given if you have a need for it.

Aside from these gifts, there are other unique capabilities, scarce resources, and greatly valued possessions that the covenant makers have. These come into play because blood covenants include the right for you to ask your covenant partner to do a favor for you. Granting the favor will require going beyond those expressly given gifts, but not beyond what you both know that the partner has the ability to do.

If your covenant partner has what you need or can do what you need done, you are permitted to ask them to give it to you or do it for you as a favor.

Four cardinal rules of covenant conduct must be followed when asking for a covenant favor.

1. When you ask your covenant partner to do a favor for you, *it must be something that the covenant partner actually has the right and ability to give to you or do for you.* It must be within the limit of their own resources to grant the favor. I can only ask for the use of your car, if you have one available. But I cannot ask for the use of your wife. Why? Because I cannot ask for something that will make any of our other covenant promises to each other or to others, null and void.

2. To draw on your mutual trust in the asking and the granting, this is vital to the whole covenant relationship; *I do not have to explain to you why I am asking the favor or make a case to compel you to do it.* It may be very difficult for you to give what I am asking for. The fact that asking for it may seem unreasonable or illogical are not to be factors influencing your decision. **Covenant is all about trust.** You must trust me to be asking for something that is important, for which I have a genuine need, and that granting the favor will do you no harm.

3. By definition, the one being asked for a favor can decide to give or not to give what has been asked for. If a partner denies the

request, he or she does not have to explain why they denied it. It may be in my own best interest not to be given what I asked for. But if you deny the favor, you just might be making a terrible and costly mistake. You might be valuing what you were asked for more than you value the relationship. ***Both partners must be doing what they choose to do of their own free will. Both must choose wisely.***

Those who truly understand blood covenant do not demand an explanation and do not refuse to comply with the request. The reason for this is the final and most important rule of conduct, it is the principle governing the process of covenanters asking a favor.

4.   Granting the favor is their free will choice, but you returning a like favor in exchange for the one granted to you is not optional. **By making the request, you both know that you are obligating yourself to do a comparable favor in return at some point in the future, up to the full extent of your own level of resources to perform.**

The analogy breaks down when the relationship being formed is based on fear rather than reciprocal love. A perverse but perfect example of the way some blood covenant "favors" work is seen in the godfather movies. An immigrant who cannot get fair treatment from the law for a grievous wrong, asks the godfather to do him a favor. The poor man knows that the godfather has far more powerful resources to draw on and can do what he asked for. The godfather plays god and grants the favor. The asker knows that he has just obligated himself with a blood oath to do something the covenant partner someday will require done in return, with no questions asked.

Covenant partners who base their relationship on love rather than fear, trust one another not to ask just to get. They ask for something that is important, and so that they can also give gladly, not reluctantly, in return.

Let's suppose you have a boat on the shoreline of Lake Galilee. It so happens that using your boat will help me more effectively teach my lesson to the large crowd gathering on the shore. I have a genuine need and so I ask you to do a favor for me. I ask you to let me use your boat.

Without questioning my need or motive, you provide the use of your boat. The boat could have been used to catch some fish, but not while I am using it. Your ability to use it while it was given to me for my use has a value. The fact is, it may not have been of much value because you had just returned from fishing and had very little to show for it. Catching fish instead of letting me use it would have been limited by the time it could have been used, the size of the boat, and the other resources you own. By asking you to do the free will favor for me, I am accomplishing two things. I am legally getting your permission to use your boat for my purposes to meet my genuine need. I am also legally obligating myself to return the favor.

The return favor is not limited to the extent of **your** ability to get fish into the boat, but rather by **my** ability to get fish into your boat. I have greater resources, so I can and I do return the boat with as many fish in it as it can possibly hold without sinking.[13] This is the covenant favor request in action. This faith-based great exchange, the giving of gifts to and favoring of one another, are the bedrock of making blood covenants.

Spoiler Alert: Because our Father God has far greater resources than we do, we are always wise to do the favors He asks of us. But the blood covenant truth just revealed is a game-changer if you caught hold of it. We now know why He would never ask us to do something beyond our ability, even if it looks that way. To do so would violate His covenant and God will never break His covenant.

---

[13] Luke 5:3-6

✠

The principal of blood covenant favor reveals why we are not to be thinking of our relationship as being one of serving a godfather out of fear, but rather a Father God out of love.

✠

This is why the widow is asked for her last measure of meal. It was not to prove that she must fear displeasing Him more than she feared death. It was so that God could legally obligate Himself to return the favor, to provide in return a lifetime of sustenance. Our Covenant Maker is intent on asking the little of us, so that He can be blessing us with more than we were asked for. Unlike the hapless immigrant, God does not regret the obligations He makes. Father God designed the whole blood covenant relationship so that He could legally obligate Himself to give far more than He asked for.

The Elements of the Blood Covenant Ceremony

The blood covenant-making ceremonies all boil down to this. There is going to be an exchange of certain things, each representing an aspect of what the two are agreeing to give to each other when asked and receive from each other when given.

Witnesses to the Exchange

There must be two or more witnesses present at the event who will represent both parties. They agree with an oath to be truthful and honest to faithfully attest to what they witnessed during the ceremony. In the future, they may need to testify to the existence of the covenant. Very importantly, they may also be asked to testify to the terms and conditions of the covenant to benefit the heirs of that covenant.

Exchange of Oaths

Prior to the ceremony, there are statements drawn up to identify what both parties are pledging and committing to do for one another. These will be the blessings that come with the keeping of the covenant. They are written, if possible, but whether in writing or not, they are always spoken. Once spoken, they cannot be reversed or annulled. This is why Isaac did not take back the blessings he spoke over Jacob even though Jacob deceived his father to get them. If you read on in his story, you will see recompense for Jacob's misdeed. He will suffer by another's deceit, but that does not change the oath of blessing Isaac spoke.

The vows are exchanged. The spoken word is their bond, so that their promises are heard by one another and by the witnesses.

Exchange of Solemn Warnings

This part is not much fun nor is it intended to be fun. It is a possibly written and always given as a strong verbal warning of what may befall the breakers of the covenant at the hands of the offended one, his family, and allies. Even the covenant breaker's own family may participate in bringing the offender to justice, lest the penalty for the offense be extracted from the family and allies of the offender. The sum of the penalties to befall the covenant breaker will leave the offender bereft of all prior benefits in particular and possibly life itself. These become the curses for breaking the covenant.

Exchange of Blood

A cut of some kind is made in the flesh of both parties. It may purposely leave a scar, but it is never harmful or life-threatening. The point is not to prove bravery or force a mark upon someone that makes them your possession. Blood representing both parties or that of an animal representing both parties is shed. It is only binding if done consensually and it is always given to the union by both parties.

The wounds may be touched to one another, or more often a small amount is placed in a cup, mixed with the juice or symbolically the blood of grapes, and both drink of it. The cut while fresh may be stained in some way, such as with ink or gun powder, to leave evidence of the cut as a sign. It may be openly displayed or done in a way that is hidden so that only the makers know of it. The blood represents the very life of the two, and the exchange or the mixing together indicates each pledges their very life to the other. If the covenant is broken, the life of the offender may be forfeited. The blood also speaks to the duration.

✠

The covenant endures as long as the lives of the covenant makers.

✠

Exchange of Names

The names of the covenant makers are augmented in a way that will represent the union of all that the makers possess, all that is held in their name. As an example, Abram's name was changed to Abra*ha*m, being augmented in two ways. A portion of the sound of the name of God, Jehov*ah*, was added to Abram, and the addition of that sound changed the name to incorporate a new identity meaningful as a result of the union. The "exalted father" became "father of a multitude." The name of God also underwent a change as He made and then reaffirmed the covenant with Abraham and his heirs, becoming "The God of Abraham, Isaac, and Jacob."

Exchange of Weapons and Clothing

When Jonathan handed his sword to David in 1 Samuel 18:3-4, he was not just giving him a present. It was very common in covenant ceremonies for there to be an exchange of weapons. This signified that the two were committed to providing physical protection to one another and coming to each other's defense.

The above passage also tells us that there was an exchange of robes that took place when David and Jonathan made a covenant. Clothes have always been both a form of covering and a way to make a statement about the one wearing them. This has been dumbed down a bit today to the extent that a person's sentiments regarding cats or coffee might be all that can be gleaned from a T-shirt they are wearing. I confess one of my favorite shirts echoes the sentiment that I might choose to reject your reality and substitute my own.[14]

In biblical times, you might be wearing more than your emotions on your sleeve. A royal robe signified that the wearer was being given the authority of the Royal who gave it. This is just one more way of signifying all that I have is yours and all that you have is mine.

The Exchange of Covenant Tokens and Erecting a Memorial Sign

When a covenant is made, tokens are exchanged or a physical monument is erected to be a lasting sign of the covenant. A token is something that stands for or serves as a sign or symbol of something else. An object can bring to remembrance what it stands for. A word for certain objects sold to tourists is a souvenir. This is a French word that literally means, *to remember*. I am a sucker for souvenirs. I love having small things in my home to help me remember important people, places, and things. While traveling, you can also exchange a piece of paper currency that stands for a value in one country for one that represents a comparable value in another country.

---

[14] A quote from the low-budget sci-fi/fantasy film The *Dungeonmaster*, popularized by Adam Savage of *Mythbusters*

A ring can be a perfect way to demonstrate that its wearers are in a covenant. In marriage, a ring is a great way to show that the partners are already spoken for and covenanted in marriage to one another.

Whole clans and nations need a prominent sign to help them to remember the covenants made by theirs and prior generations. This is where those piles of rocks come in handy. Time and again, we see in scripture that a tree, well, rock, pile of rocks, or even a mountain can bring to remembrance a covenant.

The Covenant Meal

No blood covenant ceremony would be complete without a meal. It could be an elaborate feast or as simple as sharing a piece of bread and a cup of wine. We have already noted that drinking from the same cup would take place during the ceremony. An animal gives its life, and the covenant makers and their witnesses will partake of its flesh. If they were to literally give up their own flesh and blood during the ceremony, they could not benefit from the relationship. So, they sacrificed an animal whose flesh and blood would be the substitute for the giving up of their own lives one for another. Bread was also always present, so that breaking bread together, literally, would signify their own flesh being given to sustain the life of the other.

A Closer look at the Wedding Ceremony

Earlier in the book, I demonstrated how weddings are actually blood covenant-making ceremonies. The significance of being in a blood covenant is being diluted by our society that is averse to the notion of a covenant-making God.

As you made your way through the list of exchanges above, I hope you could see how many of the parts of a traditional wedding ceremony still remain true to the fact that it should be based upon the couple making a sacred, love-based blood covenant. A healthy marriage and marriage ceremony include Father God, Jesus Christ, and the Holy Spirit in its midst.

Yet, the covenants of men and women with one another, all covenants, in fact, can only be imperfectly kept by imperfect humans. There is forgiveness in Christ for all of our covenant promises that have not been kept. No sin, no covenant-breaking, no abuse of spirit, soul, or body is too great to prevent the blood of Jesus washing from it away.

How did all of this making and breaking of covenant promises start? Is it possible that at the very beginning of our misdeeds Father God was already using the mystery of blood covenants to put in place His plan to redeem and restore all that was lost when that first set of oaths and warnings was disregarded? Read on.

Key Points: Review and Reflect

Y ou have most likely attended an event where a blood covenant is being made. Consider the elements of blood covenant ceremonies listed in this chapter. Compare these to what took place at your own wedding or one you attended.

How many elements of a covenant-making ceremony can you find?

Blood Covenant Ceremony	Wedding Ceremony
Witnesses to the Exchange	Guests of Bride and Groom are invited and asked to sit in designated areas.
Exchange of Oaths	
Exchange of Solemn Warnings	
Exchange of Blood	
Exchange of Names	
Exchange of Weapons	
Exchange of Clothing	
Exchange of Covenant Tokens	
Covenant Wine and Bread	
Covenant Feast	

You should now be able to answer the questions posed in this chapter.

> If all I have is yours and all you have is mine, how are blood covenant partners prevented from taking advantage of one another?

> What is the difference between covenant gifting and asking for a favor?

> Why is understanding this so important?

Read Romans 11:29 in the Amplified Bible:

> *For the gifts and calling of God are without repentance. For God's gifts and His call are irrevocable. [He never withdraws them when once they are given, and He does not change His mind about those to whom He gives His grace or to whom He sends His call.]*

> Why is understanding this aspect of God's covenant so important?

> When I make a request of a covenant partner, what am I obligating myself to do?

Pray and start every day thanking the Lord that our relationship with Him is not one of serving a godfather out of fear, but rather our Father God out of love.

Continue to record in your journal how the impact of what you are learning is affecting your life.

-4-

In the Beginning God, Adam, and Eve:

✠

*How does Covenant explain why Cain's
sacrifice was so seriously unacceptable?*

Many studies of the blood covenants in the Bible begin with the Abrahamic Covenant and then skip forward to the Mosaic Covenant. However, to really understand the whole picture of blood covenants, we must start where the Bible does, in the beginning.

How did all of this making and breaking of covenant promises start? It started with God committing all that He made into the care of His crowning achievement of creation: Man, or in the Hebrew, Adam. The first mention of Adam is in the account of what was created on the sixth day found in Genesis, Chapter 1. More detail is added in Chapter 2, and we must look at both to get the whole picture.

We see that Adam starts out being formed of the earth in much the same way as all other things, like every other animal, by God speaking. But then something unique happens. God uses both the spoken word that made all other things and then also adds the impartation of His own breath into Adam's nostrils. This *breath*, which is the same word in other passages translated as spirit, makes man not just a living creature, but a living spirit being.[15]

Not only did this make Adam less like all other creatures, but it also made him more like his Creator, the One who made him in His own likeness.

I believe that it was actually Jesus in His heavenly, supernatural but tangible corporal form, doing the talking and breathing. Was the Son really physically there in a way that could be sensed with our senses before He took on the more limited form of a man born of a woman? According to the New Testament, emphatically yes. The first chapter of the Gospel of John, not accidentally, also begins with the same phrase found in the first chapter of Genesis, "In the beginning." John's Holy Spirit-directed account is speaking of exactly the same timeframe as what occurred in Genesis 1.

> *In the beginning was the Word, and the Word was with God, and the Word was God. The same was in the beginning with God. All things were made by him; and without him was not any thing made that was made.* (John 1:1-3 KJV)

The King James Version word used to refer to God in Genesis is *Elohim*, actually a plural form of the word for God who also says, "Let us make man in Our image."[16] The "us" in that sentence is clearly further demonstrating the plurality of the One Triune God, referring to the total Godhead of the Father, Son, and Holy Spirit. John refers to the preexisting, walking, talking, visible portion of the Godhead who

---

[15] Genesis 2:7

[16] Genesis 1:26

will later be given the human body and name Jesus, as the Word. In the original Greek text, the term is *Logos*, literally *something spoken*.[17]

Which part of the triune God present at creation is doing the speaking? It is Jesus, aka Sir Logos, "Mr. Spoken Word." Jesus is in the Garden in a supernatural yet tangible body much like His post-resurrection body—in its functions unimpeded and unrestrained by material objects like doors, space or time, yet present on the earth. We find Him here doing the speaking and walking with Adam in the Garden, and at another time, alongside the three Hebrew children in Nebuchadnezzar's fiery furnace.[18]

When Jesus returns to the earth as a child and grows to manhood, He again walks and talks with man. He is again the tangible, felt, heard, and touched part of the unseen God. Jesus in human flesh is again carrying out on the earth the will of the Father. Jesus said, "If you have seen me, you have seen the Father."[19] Again we find Jesus to be the one doing and saying all that He says and does at the direction of the Father.

> *I am able to do nothing from Myself [independently, of My own accord—but only as I am taught by God and as I get His orders]. Even as I hear, I judge [I decide as I am bidden to decide. As the voice comes to Me, so I give a decision.* (John 5:30 AMPC)

Jesus is the purposely "made to be seen" portion of the otherwise unseen God. He is able to hear from God the Father and to have close companionship with the man made in His own likeness.

---

[17] Strong's Number g3056

[18] Daniel 3:25. Also, Google Theophany in the Bible

[19] John 14:9-10

When the first covenant was made, no blood was shed.

The One who fashioned man in His own likeness, inside and out, did so to have loving, intimate, close fellowship with a covenant partner for life. Jesus is not a disembodied voice sounding like James Earl Jones. Jesus is there in a tangible way making it all the richer and blessed to be in the Garden together. Jesus taught Adam to begin to use his speaking spirit authority by naming creatures. "Adam, what you say they are, they are." Often, a defining characteristic of that particular creation became its name. Other times, the name given helped determine the defining characteristics. We will soon see that this procedure caught on.

Jesus already demonstrated that He is the One who made all things and now He is giving Man authority over all that He created. Like all covenants, this pronouncement was intended to create a relationship that would last for as long as the covenant makers and their heirs lived. Since there was no death at the time, this was potentially an eternal covenant.

There are, of course, conditions that must be met to show that the one being entrusted with everything was indeed trustworthy, and in the truest sense, took God at His word. There were two covenant promises made that day, as with most covenants. The first promise, if there are more than one, is always the promise we like to hear about. Adam is promised a world of awesome blessings for keeping the covenant, literally. Only one statement of blessing is needed, because, in that one statement, God bequeathed to Adam absolutely everything that God created and pronounced to be good.

Next, this is followed by an equally significant, but menacing promise of dire consequences for breaking the covenant. If Adam were to take an action that would demonstrate that he no longer put his trust in the spoken word of God, he will have chosen to disobey and break the covenant. "Adam, I am going to trust you with all that I have on earth and earth itself. You must also demonstrate that you trust Me. You will do this by heeding My word not to eat of the Tree of the Knowledge of Blessing and Calamity. If you do keep the covenant, you will only know and experience Blessing. If you disobey, you will indeed immediately taste death. If you eat the fruit that will add to you knowing Calamity, the fruit you consume will consume you. You will experience, know, become intimately acquainted with, *Calamity*; catastrophe, disaster, tragedy, misfortune, sickness, and death."

The only significant element of a blood covenant not present at this short and sweet ceremony is the blood. This is because, until the fall, there was no need for the shedding of blood for any reason. The Word should have been sufficient. There was only a clear and unmistakable requirement to honor the spoken word of Mr. Spoken Word, his Creator and Friend, Jesus.

Unfortunately, we know all too well that Adam chose poorly. Eve, of course, also disobeyed, having entered into covenant by way of Adam. When God first laid down the covenant law, you may be surprised to learn that she was not created yet. Because she later came out of him, like heirs today, Eve was notified of the terms of the agreement after the fact, not at the same time as Adam. She was permitted to share what Adam already had and was to honor the rule.

There is a disconnect between what the Lord told Adam and what Eve recounted as the edict. Adam was told not to eat of it. Eve said they were told, "You shall not eat of it, and neither shall you touch it, lest you die."[20] I am speculating that Adam is the one who embellished the decree, to not so much as touch it. This may have backfired. By telling her not to touch it, he was trying to make her fear it, not just refrain from eating it out of love and obedience.

Once she saw that there was nothing to fear about its appearance and it was pleasant to touch, Eve was more easily convinced that Adam was wrong. As covenant head, Adam was the one God held most accountable. We are told in Romans that by one Man's disobedience, Adam, not by Adam and Eve's disobedience,[21] sin and death reigned in all humanity.

If Adam's offspring was the only one disobeying, the censure likely would have only involved her. But because he was the covenant maker and

---

[20] Genesis 3:3

[21] Romans 3:18

he disobeyed, ultimate responsibility for keeping or breaking the covenant, and thus bringing calamity to all creation, rested with him.

The blood is added to covenants to recover all that was lost.

The last words appearing on my screen moments ago were "calamity to all creation" that ended the last paragraph. The above phrase about recovering all that was lost was partially formed in my mind, but had not quite made it onto the digital likeness of paper. It was Tuesday at 3:26 p.m. I had begun to write at 12:03 p.m. Without warning, I heard a high-pitched ominous sound. There was no foreboding dark sky, rainstorm, wind, thunder, or lightning, but the power was immediately lost throughout all our home. The screen went dark. Curious how bad things happening and darkness go together.

I might have just lost the last three hours and twenty-three minutes of work on this chapter that lived nowhere else but in this fragile device and a likeness of what I wrote, sort of, in my altogether fallible mind. When a computer dies, anything not saved dies also. Calamity—I have known thee often before. So, I knew the fallibility of computers and had a plan in place to save my bacon and my work. Nothing was lost because before the calamity struck, I already had a backup plan in place. I literally had a backup source of power and an incremental backup process in place that allowed me to save my work even while still working. Whew!

Fortunately, at the instant of the fall, Father God was not caught by surprise. He knew of the potential depths of human fallibility and had a backup plan installed before the foundations of the earth were laid.

✠

God's backup plan was to use the mystery of blood covenants to redeem the seemingly unredeemable and to restore all that seemed irreparably lost.

✠

An excellent principle of Bible study is to know that the first account of anything happening in the Bible is always significant. The first account of any blood being shed for any reason is when animals are sacrificed by God to make a covering for His fallen man and woman.

For Adam also and for his wife the Lord God made long coats (tunics) of skins and clothed them. (Genesis 3:21 AMPC)

The blood and body of animals literally and figuratively making a covering for mankind became a ritual replayed throughout history. Animal sacrifices would be used to initiate blood covenant ceremonies, show reverence for deities they covenant with, and periodically to bring covenants to remembrance. The very first actual use of the word blood in the Bible is when Cain chose to shed Abel's blood *instead* of the blood of an animal.

As God promised, after the fall, creation reproducing itself changed in a way that is consistent with the specific penalty that fell on all fallen creation. Adam's eating the fruit of the tree of blessing and calamity brought the potential for blessing or calamity to accompany any aspect of human life. Before the fall, every single created being of all kinds was pronounced by God to be good. You do not get that designation if you are not as good as good gets. Animals were created perfect. Adam was created a perfect specimen of Man. Out of him, God created Woman—a different, yet perfect, complimentary being. Every new being entered the earth as only a blessed, perfect specimen, without defect, pain, suffering, or death.

Was the difference brought to procreation by the fall only that it would hurt more physically or was it a more dramatic change? We know this. Without the fall, every being giving life, every parent and offspring, would come out of the experience both perfect and free from pain and suffering.

*And the rib **or part of his side** which the Lord God had taken from the man He built up and made into a woman, and He brought her to the man.* (Genesis 2:22 AMPC emphasis added)

A portion of Adam, his being, a small portion of his DNA carrying cells (the word *rib* is a mistranslation) were brought *out* of him by the Lord to create Eve. Now, a small portion of a man's DNA carrying cells are placed *into* a woman to create children. Procreation was to be virtually pain-free. Sin separated Man from God's plan that would have kept the whole process completely free from calamity.

Instead, the animal kingdom and mankind must bear their offspring in a way that is ruled by the passion and the basic instincts of fallible creation. There is still the potential for every birth being a blessing, but also a potential for calamity causing unwanted offspring, sickness and disease preventing birth, or tragically damaging wanted offspring. There was more than one way that pain in childbirth was greatly multiplied. Spiritual pain can also be multiplied in the birth of a child.

How does blood covenant explain why Cain's sacrifice was so seriously unacceptable?

This potential for calamity stalking birth is certainly true of the first siblings born of woman. Calamity was not far from the door of her womb, as the enemy of our soul was watching for any opportunity to prevent a Woman's child from crushing his head.

Rather than Thing One and Thing Two,[22] Eve took her cue for naming things that came out of her from Adam. She used words she thought appropriate to name her children—names born of her experience. For better or worse, these names are important, as they often give

---

[22] **Thing One and Thing Two** are twins from <u>The Cat in the Hat</u> book by Dr. Seuss.

insight into how the children were perceived and this affected their upbringing.

The name she chose for Thing One, Cain, emphasized above all else his being the firstborn, and tied to that, his being the one destined to inherit all of their possessions.[23] What was important to her is that while the firstborn caused her greatly multiplied pain and suffering in his birth, he validated her worth by giving her husband the first-born male child. It is not a stretch to see that the woman who played a part in the fall of creation might have some self-esteem issues. Eve gained honor by producing him and took pride in his worth. As we see in the definition, the word she used to name him signifies, *this is the first child*. Literally, it also means possession, because he would be qualified as the first child to have all the possessions. Eve is a woman of few words, but she is allowed to tell us here the rationale for the name of her firstborn in her own words.

> *And Adam knew Eve as his wife, and she became pregnant*
> *and bore Cain; and she said, I have gotten and gained*
> *a man with the help of the Lord.* (Genesis 4:2-4 KJV)

The word possession is also inherent in the terms "gotten and gained." Let's review her decision. Eve: "This child is my prize possession. I have a male child who will inherit. He is the important one. His name even means firstborn and possession."

You do not have to read too far ahead in her story to see that she might have valued his birthright over his character and taught him to do the same as demonstrated by Cain. "I am the one who will possess everything by birthright, not by merit or acknowledging it as a gift of God. I need not follow all the rules. I will do what I want and no one

---

23 Strong's Concordance: h7014. קַיִן qaiyn; the same as 7013 (with a play upon the affinity to 7069); Kajin, the name of the first child, … : — Cain, Kenite(-s). AV (18)–Cain 17, Kenite 1; n pr m Cain = "possession" eldest son of Adam and Eve

else tells me what to do. I will only show contempt for anyone, even God, telling me what to do or how to do it."

Think I am reading too much into this first-born thing? Let's contrast this to the name she gave to her second born. She does not comment on him at all, apparently, it is not worth mentioning. We have to dig into the name given to find her thoughts and they are clear. Most people do not look into this, but it helps to unveil the mystery and answer the question of why Cain's sacrifice was so seriously unacceptable.

The name Abel, the Hebrew word *Habel*, is not what you may think from the similar-sounding English word, as in able to do, able worker, able body; no indeed. *Habel* literally is derived from the words for *expelled breath* and is most often translated as *vanity*.[24]

In the KJV, *Habel* is translated 73 times as vanity, 61 times as vain, and 11 times as altogether vain. To Eve, Thing Two was literally of no more value than the breath already expelled to have him; worthless, of no substance, a vapor. The pain endured to produce the firstborn had worth, but to Eve the painful time endured to give birth to the second born was spent in vain.

To us, these are hallowed names of Bible figures like Joseph or David, but to them, they were hearing the meaning and the message in the name at the same time that they heard the name spoken. If we say Joe, we do not make a value judgment. If we call him Shorty, we look to see if it is an appropriate moniker. Is it possible that Cain grows up all his life, at least during the formative first 100 years,[25] answering to the name, "Mr. First Born, my valued possession, my inheritance"? Absolutely. By contrast, Cain hears his own mother and father call his brother "Mr.

---

[24] Strong's Dictionary: h1892. לֶבֶה hebel; or (rarely in the abs.) לֶבֶה habel; from h1891; emptiness or vanity; figuratively, something transitory and unsatisfactory; often used as an adverb: — x altogether, vain, vanity.
AV (73)—vanity 61, vain 11, altogether vain 1; derived from something having the weight of vapour, and value of expelled breath.

[25] Cain was 910 years old when he died, Genesis 5:14

worthless, vain endeavor, thin air, pain in the ...." Did this have an impact on his perception of their relative value and worth? Absolutely.

The boys part company. One goes into animal husbandry. The other, who greatly values and believes he will one day own the land, tills the ground and becomes a farmer. However, at Thanksgiving sometimes you have to show up at mama's house and spend time with family members you would rather not dine with (not the case for me, but I have heard stories). They were forced to come together.

> *And Abel was a keeper of sheep, but Cain was a tiller of the ground. And in process of time, it came to pass, that Cain brought of the fruit of the ground an offering unto the Lord. And Abel, he also brought of the firstlings of his flock and of the fat thereof.* (Genesis 4:2-4 KJV)

Then as now, there was a harvest event set forth by the elders as an important time to all come together and thank God for His care, provision, and remember their blessings.

✠

They came together to honor God and thank Him for their *blood covenant* blessings!

✠

This is another covenant revelation that unveils what we cannot appreciate or understand when we view the same event without this vital perspective of blood covenant knowledge informing our hearts.

If you ever heard any Bible Story, you almost certainly heard this one about Cain and Abel, but perhaps without the benefit of covenant revelation. So, our traditional reading might go something like this.

Cain and Abel come together to give an offering to God. Both bring what they have at hand, for no reason other than to be nice and give an offering, a portion of the fruit of their labors, to God. One tends sheep, so he brings a sheep. The other tills the ground, so of course he brings a veggie plate. That seems fair and right. But if this is true, then what follows does not seem fair or right.

> *And the Lord had respect and regard for Abel and for his offering, but for Cain and his offering He had no respect or regard. So Cain was exceedingly angry and indignant, and he looked sad and depressed.* (Genesis 4:4-5 AMPC)

"Hey," we say, "that is not fair! Why did God play favorites? Why did God choose one brother's offering over the other? Poor Cain. Did they not both do their best? I thought God was no respecter of persons, but He sure did seem to here."

"Well," we are told, "we do not know why God did what He did, but you never know what God is going to do. Meat is almost always more valuable, more costly per pound, so perhaps Cain should have also brought a salad, fruit cake, and apple pie? Sometimes God does things we just do not understand."

All kidding aside, you might come away from this traditional take on the story apprehensive about your own ability to do enough to please God. You could do your best, bring it to God, and He might decide that it is just not good enough.

Now, let's rethink this after a quick look at what comes next.

> *And the Lord said to Cain, Why are you angry? And why do you look sad and depressed and dejected?* ***If you do well, will you not be accepted?*** *And if you do not do well, sin crouches at your door; its desire is for you, but you must master it.* (Genesis 4:6-7 AMPC emphasis added)

God was as outraged at Cain's behavior as Cain was by God's. But what enraged Cain? After our word study on names and having looked at their upbringing, there can be no mistake. The self-important Cain, who trusted in his being firstborn as the basis of why he was always due respect and regard, was exceedingly angry and indignant. Yet, his esteemed-as-worthless brother's offering was highly esteemed, highly regarded, and accepted by God, while Cain was given no respect and no regard.

Abel, Mr. Worthless, was accepted because he knew that the work of his hands had nothing to do with having his sins covered, his covenant honored, and the continued acceptance of God.

This was a well-known and necessary obligation to bring a sacrifice animal and shed the blood of that animal during the event set forth in the fullness of time, likely at the time of harvest. Notice, it was not just a baby sheep for God's petting zoo, it was a lamb to roast that had been slain, and the fat thereof, exactly like it will be continued to be done for millenniums. That is, until one day, God's Lamb being slain will make animal sacrifice no longer necessary. Year by year, they came to bring to their blood sacrifice to the ceremony that reminded them of the covering and blood and sacrifice God instituted when He clothed Adam and Eve.

Did Cain know this, but refused to do so anyway? Absolutely. My guess, it became unacceptable to Cain to have to go to his worthless brother and barter to pay him the acceptable fee for a lamb each year. So, this year, Cain would show that his work brought forth a bounty that was worth just as much or more than a dumb lamb. Be that accurate or not, Cain refused to come with the proper blood covenant sacrifice and substituted the work of his own hands.

✠

This is why Cain's sacrifice was so seriously unacceptable.

✠

What we do know is that Cain absolutely knew better than to bring the wrong sacrifice and that he was not deemed acceptable because his sacrifice was not acceptable. "If you do well, will you not be accepted?"

Cain gets furious, but God does not. God says there is still time. Repent and bring the proper sacrifice. If you do not, instead of your sin being removed, that sin and its menacing master is at your door, ready to pounce on you, and I will not be able to cover you.

We know Cain chose not to procure a blood sacrifice from Abel, but to shed Abel's blood instead. He did it where he actually thought he could get away with it, hiding the body in the tilled land that was his private domain. However, spilled blood has a voice God can hear, just as He can hear when a sparrow softly, imperceptibly to us, falls to the earth.

As always with God, the punishment fits the crime. Technically, there was no death sentence for murder, but Cain had defiled the land he tilled with the blood. So, God removed him from that land and from his cherished inheritance, a fate Cain felt so horrific, he said he could not bear it.

Quickly, Cain shifts back into self-preservation mode. He can no longer hide on his beloved estate; flushed out like an animal from its lair. He fears anyone who finds him will kill him for his deed even if God did not. Why? I can pose two reasons.

First, over some of those same hundreds of years of Cain's life, many other children and their children and so on have populated the earth. They are all family of slain Abel and slayer Cain. Half would seek his life as vengeance for their slain family member, and the other half for fear that if they do not, his sin and covenant curse will come upon them. Something had to be done to nip the cycle of death in the bud.

By the mercy and grace of God, He made a covenant covering for fallen Adam and Eve even though they do not deserve it. Their sin forced them from their good Garden land. Now, for their firstborn's sin, like his parents, Cain has lost his good land, his precious inheritance. Yet, God again with mercy and grace now provides a covering, an unmistakable mark to protect Cain. This mark instinctively tells others who see it that even though he is who he is and did what he did, God has spared Cain's life and they must also.

I would be interested to know your speculation on what that mark might have been. What is important is that it worked, and Cain dies of old age at 910. Whatever was done to mark him, unlike what some suppose, was not a curse. The mark was a sign of providence, covenant protection, not of a curse. His sin made Cain a marked man in one way, but God's mark in another way was a blessing that saved his life. So, again the love and the grace that is so often present but so seldom discerned in the Old Testament may be seen.

As I loved to hear Paul Harvey tell "The rest of the story,"[26] I do so here because it adds more evidence of God's much-needed love, forgiveness, and grace to the story of Eve. At the end of her story, there is an awesome footnote to her life. It gives evidence to Eve's having learned her lesson, so to speak, but more than that, to the love and grace of God.

And Adam's wife again became pregnant, and she bore a son and called his name Seth. For God, she said, has appointed for me another child instead of Abel, for Cain slew him. (Genesis 4:25 AMPC)

Eve was well aware of the heartbreaking end to Abel's life and her beloved Cain's part in it. She was aware that Abel was not worthless after all. Alas, what is done is done, what is lost is lost, but here is the rest of the story. Obviously, there were many more children born to Adam and Eve, but the Bible makes a point of footnoting the birth of Seth. God again entrusted Eve with a specific child given to her at a specific time, soon after Abel's death. This time, she actually shared the responsibility for naming him with her husband[27] and they named him Seth. They recognized him for the gift that he was, the gift of one to raise up in the slain son's stead. The name they gave to him, Seth, means *compensation*.

---

[26] Paul Harvey's The Rest of the Story, Paul Harvey Jr., 1977

[27] Genesis 4:3

Key Points: Review and Reflect

Have you seen for the first time how Adam is having fellowship in the Garden with the Son, Jesus, who appeared in the likeness of man and could be seen and heard?

How does this change the way you see the relationship between God and Man?

Why was blood absent from the first covenant between God and Man?

God made covenant directly with Man **before** Woman was created.

Why was Woman also covered by its provisions of blessing and to a lesser degree than Adam still responsible for keeping the covenant?

When did the first recorded instance of an animal being sacrificed to cover mankind take place?

Humans were only called Man and Woman prior to the fall. After that, we see the use of given names for them and their children.

Why does it matter what given names and even what nicknames are spoken over our children?

Why did God not respect the offering brought by Cain?

Was this an eye-opener for you?

Continue to record in your journal how the impact of what you are learning is affecting your life.

-5-

Abraham

*Unto Abraham: If we knew what Abraham
knew, could we now do what Abraham did?*

As we continue to unveil the secrets of the blood covenants that
unfold after Adam and Eve, we turn our attention to the story
of the covenant between God and Abraham. This is the single most
important Old Testament story to see from the perspective of unveiling
since it's rooted and grounded in the making and keeping of blood covenants. Let's start by looking at the unimaginable request God makes
of Abraham.

> *And it came to pass after these things, that God did
> tempt Abraham, and said unto him, Abraham: and
> he said, Behold, here I am. And He said, Take now thy
> son, thine only son Isaac, whom thou lovest, and get thee
> into the land of Moriah; and offer him there for a burnt
> offering upon one of the mountains which I will tell thee
> of.* (Genesis 22:1-2 KJV)

Abraham is to be the instrument of his own son's death and then trust God to raise him from the dead. Also, he is not to just do it someday, but now. Furthermore, Abraham will not be able to just symbolically cut Isaac's flesh with a knife, he would have to confirm that the cut shed sufficient blood so that the one sacrificed would have died on the altar. Then his son's body would have to be burned to ashes.

> *By faith Abraham, when he was put to the test [while the testing of his faith was still in progress], had already brought Isaac for an offering; he who had gladly received and welcomed [God's] promises was ready to sacrifice his only son, of whom it was said, Through Isaac shall your descendants be reckoned. For he reasoned that God was able to raise [him] up even from among the dead. Indeed in the sense that Isaac was figuratively dead [potentially sacrificed], he did [actually] receive him back from the dead.* (Hebrews 11:17-19 AMPC)

Before we go on, let me provide the covenant principle that underscores the last statement above. Although it had not already taken place, Abraham did actually receive Isaac back from the dead. As far as Abraham was concerned, when did Isaac die? The answer is three days before the sacrifice was to be performed, on that morning, he told his servants to prepare the donkey for the three-day journey. The moment Abraham spoke a command and took action to do what his covenant partner had asked of him, there was no going back. As far as Abraham was concerned, his son was already dead.

Recapping, God's great promises included that only through this one specific firstborn of Sarah, Isaac, whom he loved, Abraham's descendants would outnumber the stars Abraham could count. Then that same God, who made that promise, asks Abraham to take that son on a three-day journey to a mountain top and kill that son. Not kill the son because he was guilty of anything, but rather as a sacrifice to God as if he was simply an animal.

How could anyone become so close in his walk with God, so perfect, so holy, so unwaveringly full of faith, so selfless, and so determined to give all he cared about in life to God? And not out of fear of death, but willingly? God is putting Abraham to an impossible test. Can he do it? Can anyone do it? What if his faith is not strong enough? What if he fails to follow through or God does not do the impossible?

Apart from the full and complete understanding of blood covenant (not just that part you might get from fearing to break a covenant lest you die), it would appear what God is asking Abraham to do is a bit unreasonable. He is not just asking him to leave his comforts of home to go to the mission field, or enter full-time ministry, or to take a vow of poverty, or be temporarily separated from family. Apparently, Abraham was willing to prove how much he loved God and how much blind faith he had by agreeing to kill the son of promise with no questions asked.

We might understandably marvel at his faith, but we also have to answer this question. How many of us think we could have the faith it would take to do what Abraham did, unquestioning, unflinching, without delay, to intentionally kill our own child for God? It clearly appears to say God was testing him with something so hard to do, that by passing the test, Abraham will prove his devotion was greater than any other man. He would thereby prove himself worthy to receive what God had promised to give him. Would he be up to the test? The test purposely included a three-day journey to the place of sacrifice so that he could consider, dread, and ponder his decision; perhaps to prove it was no crime of passion or impulse. In the end, would he be unwilling or unable to do it and risk God cutting him off from all the other promises?

Before I received the insight I am about to share with you, I had some of this misguided and inaccurate questioning severely clouding my own thoughts. This story was not at all inspiring to me. It was quite the opposite. I confess that I did not understand the true nature of God or the deep mystery of blood covenants. I was taught in church to love

God and also to fear Him, with the scales more often tipping towards the latter. If I did not measure up, I was to fear His punishment now and His wrath in the coming apocalypse. I was taught to fear that if I was not living righteously and good enough, keeping the Sabbath holy, and keeping all of the Ten Commandments, I would not deserve to be raptured. I might be left behind.

If God asked me to do something that was as hard for me to do as what Abraham did, would I choose to please God or please myself? I might lose my salvation if I did not repent of backsliding and respond to the altar call to "get right with God" and be a more righteous and holy person like Abraham.

I can understand a healthy fear of not accepting the offer of salvation, but I was having these fear issues even though I was saved, born again, believed the Bible, and tried to live right as best I could.

✠

**I was afraid if I tried to get as close to God as Abraham did,
I would also be asked to make unreasonable sacrifices
to prove my worthiness and I would fail to measure up.**

✠

Traditionally, we have seen some of the promises of God in response to our faith as amazing. Yet, perhaps only attainable as a reward for a life of holiness, sacrifice, and spiritual growth requiring faith greater than what we can quite muster. We might shy away from the story of Abraham's faith because we doubt we could have the faith it took to kill his son. We fear God may test our faith in a way too hard for us to do.

Then, the breakthrough came that would change my life. I heard the still, soft, but unmistakable voice of God, whether audibly or only on the inside I cannot say. He first got my attention with this phrase:

**"If you knew what Abraham knew, you could easily
have done what Abraham did."**

Then He continued, "I am going to reveal to you how to not stagger at obtaining by faith the promises of the Bible. You used to stagger at the faith of Abraham. I am going to teach you how to have the faith of Abraham. I am going to teach you how to not stagger at My promises the same way I caused Abraham to not stagger and to have sufficient faith to be able to obtain that which I promised to Him. I will cause you to comprehend what it means for Me to have made a blood covenant with you; a new and better one than the one I made with Abraham."

I discovered that the relationship between God and Abraham was a love-prompted, mutually beneficial, blood-covenant relationship. The righteousness Abraham enjoyed was not based upon his perfection or his works before *or after* entering into the covenant. Perfect right standing with God was a gift that was accounted to him. That means it was given to him as a byproduct or benefit of having entered into the blood covenant with God. The covenant terms were simple. God would make beneficial promises to Abraham. In return, only one thing was required of Abraham. Abraham was required to simply believe that God would not break His covenant.

✠

Hours of sacrificial prayer, fasting, reading through the Bible in a year, working in the church, trying to get good enough, right enough, penitent enough, doing enough good for others, keeping every commandment and dietary law, being holy enough, loving your enemies enough, forgiving others enough, and acting humble enough will not cause you to have the faith of Abraham.

✠

Your works will not impart great faith in Bible promises. These are not the path to having what is not based upon what you can do. It was not what he did prior to being asked that prepared or qualified Abraham to be able to do the hard thing that God asked him to do. Abraham teaches us that we can have the great faith he came to have the same way he came to have it. *If we knew what Abraham knew, could we now do what Abraham did?* So, what did Abraham come to know?

What Abraham Knew

Long before making a blood covenant with God, Abraham strongly believed in the benefits of being in a blood covenant relationship with men. After making a covenant with God, Abraham still continued to make covenants with men as needed. In the passage of Genesis just prior to the verse where God asked Abraham to do a rather difficult covenant favor for Him, we see Abraham cut a blood covenant with Abimelech to avoid escalation of a deadly confrontation with Philistia.[28]

✠

It is very important to know God did not cut a covenant with Abram until many years after he was instructed to leave his homeland and became a wealthy man.

✠

During all of the earlier chapters in Genesis, you will see Abraham referred to as Abram. The name change came much later. God would tell Abram in a vision what to do next. Abram sensed this was a spiritual encounter with a higher being, so he decided to follow the instructions given by the Voice. The Voice would tell Abram where to go and Abram would see that blessings multiplied every time he did as instructed. The Voice of God also said that in addition to the material blessings, He would also give him the land he traveled in, and that He would make of Abram a great nation, not just a large family. As the years went on, Abram gained great wealth in land and possessions, becoming famously

---

28 Genesis 21: 25-34 (AMPC)

and enviably prosperous, so much so that he would even become a blessing to others.[29]

All we have up to this point is God saying in visions to go where he was led to go. Then Abram would pitch a tent, build an altar, and perhaps dig a well, thus, putting his mark on the land.

So far, so good. Abram becomes rich and prosperous in almost every way imaginable simply on the basis of doing what God said to do and going where He said to go in the visons. Almost. The part about a large family that would eventually grow to the size of a small nation was part of the original promise. However, after many years of this relationship, it was not happening. There was no firstborn child to inherit it. This was a big problem in his mind and it was getting late in his life. Abram was bold enough to resolve to confront the issue on the next occasion of God visiting him in a vision. Sure enough, the Lord opened up the conversation in a way that was consistent with all the other visions, on a rather happy note.

AFTER THESE things, the word of the Lord came to Abram in a vision, saying, Fear not, Abram, I am your Shield, your abundant compensation, and your reward shall be exceedingly great. (Genesis 15:1 AMPC)

Abram stops God right there, and says, paraphrasing, "Hey, what is the point of giving me anything more when You have failed to do what You first said You would do for me? Specifically, You said You would give me a family so large that it was the size of a nation, and after all this time I do not have even a single child. I am going to have to leave all this stuff to a servant from Damascus!"

And Abram said, Lord God, what can You give me, since I am going on [from this world] childless and he who

---

[29] Genesis 12:2

shall be the owner and heir of my house is this [steward]
Eliezer of Damascus?

Abram almost implied that God really did not care about what happened to him or forgot what He promised. It sure reminds me of his children many years hence, perhaps it is in the DNA. Moses delivers the children of Abraham out of Egypt because of their covenant, but instead of thanking him, at every bump in the road, they said, "Why did you bother to take us out of Egypt, and lead us into a dessert where we are all going to die? Were there not enough graves in Egypt?"

It is so telling of their relationship that Abram felt comfortable enough with God, to contend with Him for what he wanted. Instead of getting furious, God's response is to double down on those promises and says, paraphrasing, "Did I say a nation full of descendants? Come over here. You see all of these stars? Just try to count them. See the grains of sand in the desert? Your descendants are going to outnumber these!"[30]

Up until now, Abram simply believed the God voice in his visions would do what He said and God honored that. But now, there was too great a thing to believe and an equally great desire to believe it. Bold again, Abram says, "I am a man and You are the supernatural being I hear speaking to me in visions, but how can I really know beyond the shadow of a doubt, that You will do what You promised?"

God says to Himself, again paraphrasing, "I thought you would never ask!" God is going to do the one thing Abraham knows to the core of his being, to the deepest part of his humanity, the one thing Abram could trust as the answer to the question, "How can I really know You will do what You promised?" There is one thing that Abram can put all of his hope and trust in and that is precisely when God lets Abram know that He is going to cut a blood covenant with him.

---

[30] Genesis 15:4-5

*And He said to him, Bring to Me a heifer three years old,
a she-goat three years old, a ram three years old, a turtle-
dove, and a young pigeon.*

*And he brought Him all these and cut them down the
middle [into halves] and laid each half opposite the other...*
(Genesis 15:9-10 AMPC)

Without another word, Abram knew that God just told him to
prepare a sacrifice for an all-encompassing blood-covenant ceremony,
which is why he knew exactly how to prepare the sacrifice animals. This
particular variation on the common theme of identity with the animals
in a blood-covenant ceremony goes as follows. Those who are agreeing
to keep their promises will do something to show the depth of their
commitment to their covenant partner. In this case, they will walk in a
figure-eight pattern into the path of blood between the two halves of
the animals, then circle around to walk through them again. It is interesting that this forms a figure-eight pattern that becomes the symbol for
infinity. This is saying these animals stand in for my own being. I have
their blood on me, and if I break my covenant promise my life, like that
of these animals, will be forfeited.

*And [God] said to Abram, Know positively that your
descendants will be strangers dwelling as temporary residents in a land that is not theirs [Egypt], and they will
be slaves there and will be afflicted and oppressed for 400
years. But I will bring judgment on that nation whom
they will serve, and afterward they will come out with
great possessions. And you shall go to your fathers in peace;
you shall be buried at a good old (hoary) age. And in the
fourth generation they [your descendants] shall come back
here [to Canaan] again, for the iniquity of the Amorites is
not yet full and complete. When the sun had gone down*

and a [thick] darkness had come on, behold, a smoking oven and a flaming torch passed between those pieces. On the same day the Lord made a covenant (promise, pledge) with Abram, saying, to your descendants I have given this land... (Genesis 15:13-18 AMPC)

This was a brilliant literal way to have the unseen God manifest Himself in a way that is sufficient to demonstrate His life was on the line and that the Voice is now also participating in a material way, showing Himself to be with his covenant partner. A few years later, He would do it again. God would show Himself present with the Children of Abraham during their journey to the Promised Land as a pillar of smoke by day and fire by night.

By making a blood covenant, Abram knew God would do what He promised. A promise in a covenant is not a wish-to-do, a hope-to-do, or if I can get around to it, like I promise to come over sometime. A broken promise in a blood covenant could result in the death of the covenant promise-breaker. Knowing this, Abram was confident that he could now believe God would do what He said He would do. Notice also, at this point, God had not asked His covenant partner to do anything in return other than to believe Him, *so only God was required to walk through the blood.*

When you read on to Genesis 17, you will see that after a certain amount of time, after Abram made a few poor choices including trying to take a short cut to fatherhood with Sarah's servant, God returns. Because Abram's covenant was by grace rather than under a covenant of Laws, Abram's high crimes and misdemeanors did not disqualify him from the promises.

The time is approaching for the promised birth, so now the covenant is cut deeper at a second ceremony. God adds here another element so common in covenant-making. God took a part of His name, the *"ah"* sound from Jehov*ah*, and added it to Abram's name. Abram becomes Abr*ah*am. By adding that to the name, this also changed its meaning from *Exalted Father* to *Father of Nations*. This is part of the process of instilling and bolstering faith in the covenant promises God made. Everyone is now calling him Father of Nations before he has had his first child.

An exchange of names is not complete if only one name is changed. From this point forward, God agreed to also include His covenant partners' name(s) in His. God will now be known as the God of Abraham. Later, the same covenant is reconfirmed to be made with the heir of Abraham, Isaac. Later the same covenant is reconfirmed with Isaac's son, Jacob. It is at that point, God is referred to in Scripture as the God of Abraham, Isaac, and Jacob.

A little bit later, still a final covenantal name change takes place. The man who once was accurately named by his mom Jacob, *supplanter*, needs a new identity. The struggle with his brother is over, Jacob won and became the next covenant head of Abraham's descendants. At that very same time, there is one who is supernatural in appearance, clearly representing God, who in a physical form comes to meet with Jacob. The one who previously struggles with his brother for his father's blessing, now contends with God for His blessing. How appropriate is the new name Jacob earns in this encounter. He, his descendants, and their nation will now be aptly known as Israel, *Contends with God*.[31]

Returning to the covenant ceremony where Abraham's name is changed, this time there is added to their covenant one more important step in creating the identity of the Covenant People descended from Abraham. Now, Abraham has a task that is part of the ceremony. Abraham will make a mark of the covenant in his flesh and the flesh of every male child born to him with circumcision. It is not an outward public mark for all to see the evidence of a powerful covenant maker's mark. It is a hidden mark for them to personally remember their identity as Children of Abraham and heirs covered by that covenant.

---

[31] Genesis 32:24-28

Now God asks Abraham to do a Favor

Almost everything church tradition or veiled human understanding led us to surmise from the reading of the passage where God asks Abraham to sacrifice his son is incorrect. Surmise is an excellent word to use because it means to infer, derive, or imagine something based upon incomplete evidence. What happened is quite correctly stated. It is what **we thought was happening** that to a great extent is wrong. We drew our conclusions with incomplete evidence. I have heard many sermons, read commentaries, and myself drawn inaccurate conclusions about these things. Here are some of the things we might have gotten wrong.

- What God's motives were for putting Abraham to the test.

- What it really meant to put Abraham to the test.

- Abraham's reason for not trying to reason with God as to why.

- Whether or not there was any fear or doubt involved on the part of Abraham when God asked him to kill his son.

- What enabled Abraham to be willing and able to kill his son.

- Why it was not an unreasonable ask by God.

- The inference that if you want to draw close to God you will have to prove your spiritual worthiness, and prove to also be worthy to receive from God like Abraham.

- We must blindly sacrifice everything to prove that we are worthy to receive what God promises us in His Word.

- What the real reason is behind God asking Abraham to kill Isaac.

To some extent the mystery surrounding God's plan was entirely on purpose. The life-changing, mind-changing, awesome import of these passages cannot be fully understood without two things.

✠

We must unveil the mystery of what it is in their blood covenant that guides every move of God and Abraham. It is only the record of the New Testament that can complete our understanding of what really happened in this Old Testament story.

✠

The first thing I will shed light on is the issue of God's motives for "putting Abraham to the test." A common notion is that God was wanting to either know or show whether or not Abraham was *worthy* enough to be given the covenant blessing of his descendants being innumerable, and or *worthy* enough to be given the Promised Land as his inheritance. Does Abraham love God enough to give such a great sacrifice? Is Abraham good enough? Does he have enough faith to sacrifice everything, forsake everything to gain the great promises?

Something crucial is missing here. There is no quid pro quo. Read the transcript! Which is to say, there is no statement in these passages of scripture saying, "If you do this for Me, *only then* I will do what I had promised for you." There is no withholding of promises, there is no, "If you do not do this for me, I will not do that for you."

Gifts offered in a covenant are not renegotiable. You cannot add a requirement later to receive a gift that was in the original agreement. There is no renegotiation of the contract here. If Abraham does what was asked of him, it will only prove Abraham believed God would do what He already said He would do. God also did not preface the request with, "If you love Me, you will do this." All God did is to ask Abraham to do it, without any explanation as to why or the consequences if he chose not to do it. If there was not the option to choose, then He was not asking for something to be done consensually. Yet, we now know that in covenants, what you ask must be consensual.

✠

**God was asking Abraham to do a favor, not perform
a heroic act that would either qualify or disqualify him
from being given what God had previously promised.**

✠

That may at first surprise you. In order for this chapter to be understood, it is important that you have carefully read the part in the prior chapter dealing with asking your covenant partner to do a favor for you. Covenant makers are allowed to give things to their partners, and if they do, these are given with no strings attached. Aside from that, they can also ask their partner to do a favor for them.

1. When you ask your blood covenant partner to do a favor for you, it must be something that the blood covenant partner actually has the right and ability to do for you. It must be within the limit of their own resources to grant the favor you ask of them.

2. To draw on your mutual trust in the asking and the granting, it is vital to the whole blood covenant relationship, that I do not have to explain to you why I am asking the favor or make a case to compel you to do it. It may be very difficult for you to give what I am asking for. The fact that asking for it may seem unreasonable or illogical are not to be factors influencing your decision.

3. By definition, a consensual request means that the one who is being asked for a favor can decide to give or not to give what has been asked for. If a partner denies the request, that one also does not have to explain why they denied it. **Both partners must be doing what they choose to do ungrudgingly and of their own free will.**

The fact is, God was asking His blood covenant partner to do a very important and very much needed favor for Him. This truth makes a fatal blow to every human effort to explain the testing part of this being a way to determine whether or not Abraham was good enough, faithful enough, holy enough, or any other way so perfect and worthy to now receive what was **previously** promised. What was already promised, was already his. Abraham was not required to be perfect or even good to get it. So, why change the terms of the agreement now? It was not even about testing Abraham. It was about Abraham doing what God wanted and needed him to do for Him. The test was simply to prove what God already knew—Abraham was willing and able to do the favor God asked of him.

✠

Abraham believed God was able to do what He said He would do, *regardless* of what Abraham did. Even if Abraham killed the son of promise, Isaac, he knew that God would still somehow or another honor His blood-covenant promise. God would give him nations full of descendants from Isaac, dead or alive.

✠

This testing must be seen in the right perspective to make any covenant sense at all. If there are several coins that look like gold, but if I know nothing about them, I would want to have a test done to prove what they are worth. The result is not at all a foregone conclusion. However, if a coin is one that I bought directly from the US Mint, I am confident that it is gold, not gold-plated silver that only looks good on the outside. If I want to sell my coin to you, are you going to take my word for its value when you do not even know me? It is in both our best interests that at the time of purchase, I have a third-party witness, an accredited laboratory, certify with a test of the metal, that it is what I already know it to be. The test is so that the sale of the coin will hold up in court if the value of the coin is ever questioned. The test does not change my confidence in the coin, it only proves its needed element was in it at the time of the transaction.

Now, let's apply covenant truth to dispel myths and to demystify all the questions raised earlier in the chapter.

What was God's motive for putting Abraham to the test?

It was to demonstrate to heaven and earth that Abraham already had in him the one element that qualified him to be able to do what was asked of him.

What qualified Abraham to pass the test?

It was not about Abraham having enough of his own righteousness, holiness, or power to do anything; he was only required to demonstrate that he simply believed that God was able to do what God promised He would do. Abraham believed God and it was counted unto him for righteousness (Romans 4:3 KJV).

Why did Abraham have absolutely no fear or doubt that God would do what He promised to do?

Because God cut a blood covenant with Abraham, he knew that God had to keep His promises or cease to exist. Abraham had no doubt that God would, if need be, raise his son from the ashes. He told the servants at the base of the mountain, "the boy and I will return."

What was Abraham's reason for *not* trying to reason with God?

God asked Abraham to do a covenant-partner favor for Him. It was none of his business to ask his covenant partner why He wanted the favor. To do so, and then base your decision on the answer, is to make you the judge and puts your partner on trial. You either grant the favor He asks out of love or you do not.

What enabled Abraham to be more than willing to do what appears to be an unreasonable ask by God?

It only appears to be unreasonable, but reasoning does not play a part in responding out of love to an earnest and important requested favor. God had done so much for him; he was only too glad to actually be able to do something for the God who now actually needed something from Abraham. Understanding the consequences of God breaking His blood covenant promise is what enabled Abraham to believe God would keep His promise even if Abraham killed his son.

What was the real reason God asked Abraham to kill his son?

The answer to this question is the life-changing, mind-changing, awesome importance of these passages. We now know there was more going on than just testing Abraham's merit. Some readers likely have a partial answer already. God asked Abraham to sacrifice his son because at a future point He would do likewise, right? Yes, but there is so much more to it. You just do not want to miss what I am about to reveal.

Think about this. At the time God asks Abraham to sacrifice his son, no one on earth or in heaven, or in the darkest regions of hell, knows why. And I mean no one. The *assumption* is, that this is just a very hard test that God demanded that Abraham pass to prove he was worthy to receive all that God has promised. Yet, the terms of his covenant with God say that Abraham did not have to be perfect in the first place. Abraham believed God and it was *accounted* to him as being righteous. Gifts previously promised cannot be renegotiated to require something not in the original agreement be done to earn them, or they are not gifts. So, if it is not to prove Abraham's spiritual worthiness and it was not so that he could qualify to receive what he was previously promised as a free gift, then what was it for?

The test helped God to hide in plain sight what He was really doing. We know from scriptures spanning the Old and New Testaments, the enemy was always looking for the man born of woman that God said would crush his head. This was particularly true when one of these men started hearing from God and doing mighty exploits.

Imagine the confusion on the dark side. This man Abraham is being highly favored, becoming rich and finally having a child in a much unexpected, miraculous way. Maybe this "child of promise," Isaac, is the one the minions of hell should fear, maybe this is the one they needed to target for a premature death. Then the father is asked to do the job for them! Maybe Isaac failed to turn out right and God was going to have this one killed, so that another could take his place. Maybe Isaac would raise from the ashes and prove that he will be the one who is destined to destroy Satan. No, wait. Just as he was about to do the deed, Abraham is stopped in mid-swing. God called it all off. Oh, it was just a test of Abraham's devotion, nothing more. The enemy shook his head, uttered a sigh of relief, and thought, nothing to see here.

Nothing the enemy could see, but a great deal for us to see. Part of the answer cannot be seen until it is too late for the enemy to follow the trail of what is about to really happen in the Old Testament to its conclusion in the New Testament. As you come to know the mystery of the blood covenants, you will know why God asked Abraham to grant Him this favor. Here are the last crucial things you need to know about asking a favor of your covenant partner.

You cannot ask a partner to grant a favor that is beyond their capacity to do what you ask. It will not be a matter of can I or can I not do what you asked. It is a matter of will I or will I not do what you ask. It also must be done altogether willingly, without holding back and not begrudgingly.

Granting the favor is their free-will choice, **but you returning a like favor in exchange, in due time, is not optional**. By making the request, you both know that you are obligating yourself to do a comparable favor in return at some point in the future, up to the full extent of *your own* level of resources to perform.

✠

The reason God asked Abraham to sacrifice his son for Him, was to obligate Himself to do exactly what He asked for, a legally binding in heaven and on earth blood covenant honoring a return favor; to the full extent of God's level of resources and ability to perform.

✠

Let's take a much closer look at Genesis Chapter 22 where we will now see exactly what God asked Abraham to do. Then, as only He could do, obligate Himself to return the favor.

> *[God] said, Take now your son, your only son Isaac, whom you love, and go to the region of Moriah; and offer him there as a burnt offering upon one of the mountains of which I will tell you.*

- God will sacrifice His only Son.

- Not just any son, but the only Son, the one whom He loved.

- The region of Moriah includes what would become Jerusalem.

- The mountain was Mount Zion.

> *So Abraham rose early in the morning, saddled his donkey, and took two of his young men with him and his son Isaac;*

- Jesus will arrive in Jerusalem on a donkey.

- There would be two witnesses (two is the minimum blood-covenant requirement) testifying that Jesus came willingly to the place where He would be sacrificed.

> *He split the wood for the burnt offering and then began the trip to the place of which God had told him.*

- Abraham took with him split wood upon which to lay his son. Jesus will lay upon wood that was split to form a cross and then be raised upon it.

On the third day, Abraham looked up and saw the place in the distance.

- Because Abraham swore to kill his son before leaving home, his son will be dead to the father for three days. Jesus will be dead, separated from His Father, for three days.

And Abraham said to his servants, Settle down and stay here with the donkey, and I and the young man will go yonder and worship and come again to you.

- There will be more than two witnesses testifying that Jesus said that He would be killed and that after His death, in three days, He would be raised from the dead.

Then Abraham took the wood for the burnt offering and laid it on [the shoulders of] Isaac his son, and he took the fire (the firepot) in his own hand, and a knife; and the two of them went on together.

- Both sons carried the wood for their own sacrifice on their own shoulders.

And Isaac said to Abraham, My father! And he said, Here I am, my son. [Isaac] said, See, here are the fire and the wood, but where is the lamb for the burnt sacrifice? Abraham said, My son, God Himself will provide a lamb for the burnt offering. So the two went on together.

- The sacrifice will be of a lamb. It will either be Isaac or another, at that point in time, Abraham did not know which, but as he said, he knew the lamb would be provided. God provided His own Son to be the lamb for His return favor sacrifice, the lamb that was preplanned to be slain before the foundations of the earth.[32]

---

[32] Revelation 13:8

When they came to the place of which God had told him, Abraham built an altar there; then he laid the wood in order and bound Isaac his son and laid him on the altar on the wood.

- When they reach the place of His sacrifice, Jesus is then laid upon and also bound to the wood that would become the altar for His sacrifice.

And Abraham stretched forth his hand and took hold of the knife to slay his son. But the Angel of the Lord called to him from heaven and said, Abraham, Abraham! He answered, here I am. And He said, do not lay your hand on the lad or do anything to him; for now I know that you fear and revere God, since you have not held back from Me or begrudged giving Me your son, your only son. Then Abraham looked up and glanced around, and behold, behind him was a ram caught in a thicket by his horns. And Abraham went and took the ram and offered it up for a burnt offering and an ascending sacrifice instead of his son! So Abraham called the name of that place The Lord Will Provide. And it is said to this day, on the mount of the Lord it will be provided.

- And indeed, on Mount Zion, the mount of the Lord, God returned the favor.

Key Points: Review and Reflect

As far as Abraham was concerned, when does covenant awareness tell us Isaac died?

Why will your righteous works not impart to you the great faith Abraham had?

What enabled Abraham to be more than willing to do what appears to be an unreasonable ask by God ungrudgingly?

Name two deeper and more important reasons that God tested Abraham by asking him to kill his son.

Is there something difficult Father God is asking you to do?

You now know that like Abraham, you will not be asked to do something you are not able to do. Also, Abraham was able to believe that God would keep His promises because he knew that he had a blood covenant with God. You have a new and better blood covenant than Abraham.

If you now know what Abraham knew, could you now do what Abraham did?

Continue to record in your journal how the impact of what you are learning is affecting your life.

-6-

King David

✠

What was David's secret to his every success?
Why do we need to know who Mephibosheth is?

Hundreds of years pass between the story of Abraham and the story of King David. Yet, one thing remains. Blood covenant truth continued to be the foundation and cornerstone of the stories of the mighty exploits of the heroes of faith. The God of Abraham, Isaac, and Jacob has proven Himself trustworthy and has kept His promises. Jacob is renamed Israel and God will now be known through the balance of the Old Testament as the God of Israel, first denoting the man Israel, and then his heirs, the Children of Promise. God would deliver the bloodline of Abraham as promised from Egypt. God also provided for them as they sojourned in the desert and led them triumphantly into the Promised Land.

The children of Israel entered the land and conquered the inhabitants who served other gods such as Baal. At first, the nation was a theocracy. That term simply means that God was their ultimate ruler rather than a human king. Assisting God in leading the nation were a series of prophets and judges, with mixed results. Unfortunately, they often chose poorly. The more they wanted to be like other nations who had strong, tall, imposing human figures as their kings, the more poorly they chose. This culminated in Israel choosing Saul to be their official first human King. The two defining qualities they admired him for were that Saul was handsome in appearance and physically taller than others. In hindsight, we will see just how ridiculously shortsighted they were.

> *Kish had a son named Saul, a choice young man and handsome; among all the Israelites there was not a man more handsome than he. He was a head taller than any of the people.* (1 Samuel 9:2 AMPC)

If there is one thing we learned from Abraham, it is that his success in life depended entirely on believing in the capabilities of his covenant partner God, not in his own perfection, strength, appearance, virility, or hat size. God's message is shouted over and over through the lives of His covenant partners. Because they remembered their covenant, slaves were able to defeat a pursuing and rather well-equipped Egyptian army. Armed with only the ability to walk and talk, His covenant children also brought down the walls of a fortified city. A covenant man named Gideon went from hiding in a well where he was thrashing wheat fearful of being robbed by enemy sentries, to overthrowing and taking the spoils from entire opposing armies.

Nevertheless, when choosing a king, the children of Israel chose poorly. God's choice will prove this out, while also proving why he was God's choice.

✠

Saul trusted in his own strength. David trusted in the blood covenant that defined his personal relationship with the God of Israel.

✠

Blood Covenant in the Morning of David's Life

> *Surely goodness and mercy shall follow me all the days of
> my life: and I will dwell in the house of the Lord forever.*
> (Psalm 23:6 KJV)

There being little else to do with his spare time in the wilderness, David honed his skills as a singer, songwriter, and worship leader for an audience of sheep. Later in life, he will reprise these roles for a larger audience.

David learned how to praise and trust his covenant God while entrusted with the care of the family business. He was not just a hired hand; David knew that the animals in his care were their source of sustenance and a part of their family inheritance. He was only a young adolescent, in the morning of his life. David was the last born, not the firstborn. His oldest and strongest brothers were proudly serving on the battlefield with Saul while he, being the youngest and smallest, was at home tending sheep.

Yet faithful in little, he would be given much. The young man was already able to prevail with the help of God against the largest and fiercest animals that tried to take his sheep as prey. In some cases, his sharpshooter skills with a slingshot were used. At other times, he ripped a lamb from the teeth of a lion with his bare hands.

> *And David said to Saul, Your servant kept his father's
> sheep. And when there came a lion or again a bear and
> took a lamb out of the flock, I went out after it and smote
> it and delivered the lamb out of its mouth; and when it
> arose against me, I caught it by its beard and smote it and
> killed it.* (1 Samuel 17:34-35 AMPC)

How did David come to have the confidence to do what he did in the field of sheep which then prepared him to do the same in the field of battle? Well, it was not by playing Candy Crush. David put his confidence in Israel's blood covenant God. Many of his Psalms evidence David's knowing the *Pentateuch*, the first five historical books of the Bible attributed to Moses. The biblical record of his people told David exactly what the basis was for the success of Abraham, Isaac, and Jacob. They trusted the covenant promises of God and worshipped the God of those promises. Their flocks grew large and were protected from man and beast by the covenant-making God. It was not lost on David that all of these great men also had started out in life tending sheep and ended up shepherding the nation.

Meanwhile, his older brothers, who put pride in their position and station in life, constantly belittled their little brother and his shepherding duties. David comes to them at the battlefield at his father's request. He is dutifully delivering care packages for the troops. Instead of thanking him, the eldest takes the opportunity to again try to put him in what they perceive to be his place.

> *Now Eliab his eldest brother heard what he said to the men; and Eliab's anger was kindled against David and he said, Why did you come here? With whom have you left those few sheep in the wilderness? I know your presumption and evilness of heart; for you came down that you might see the battle.* (1 Samuel 17:28 AMPC)

Really? "Few sheep" would suggest that since there were so few there would be no need for him to stay with them anyway. I am sure there were more than a few. "In the wilderness" suggests it is a lowly place to be put. But doing this work in the wilderness, among wild beasts, does that not suggest that it is a harder place to do your shepherding? So often, we see that the one who is really presumptive and evil at heart is the one making the accusations!

What riled his brother up again to the point of having an episode of DDS (Davidic Derangement Syndrome)? It was the fact that David came just at the right time to see and hear Goliath come out again and taunt them. All of them, including his brothers, were cowering. None of them were willing to take up the challenge, even though a great deal of wealth and favor would be heaped upon anyone who did answer the challenge. What wealth, what favor? That is what David wanted to know.

> *And David said to the men standing by him, What shall be done for the man who kills this Philistine and takes away the reproach from Israel? For who is this uncircumcised Philistine that he should defy the armies of the living God? And all the men of Israel, when they saw the man, fled from him, terrified. And the Israelites said, Have you seen this man who has come out? Surely he has come out to defy Israel; and the man who kills him the king will enrich with great riches, and will give him his daughter and make his father's house free [from taxes and service] in Israel.* (1 Samuel 17:24-26 AMPC)

This is where I want to make sure you see that David's response to all of this is what one says when understanding his covenant promises and puts his trust specifically in the power of his blood covenant with God.

David is not presumptive, greedy, or acting unbefitting a humble servant of God. It is not at all inappropriate to expect and gladly accept the wealth and riches freely offered when you do what being in covenant prompts you to do even if not rewarded. David did not say, nor should he say, "Hey, no problem king, I will do it for free, for I am a humble servant of the Lord." Not only wealth, but your whole household including your parents, brothers, and your decedents free from taxes in perpetuity? Send me in, coach! All this and getting the king's daughter, too? Well, that does not sound so bad either (even if Saul turned out to be a terrible father-in-law!)

All of this would be his in exchange for simply and fearlessly relying on the God of his covenant. He was confident that he would be able to triumph over any *uncircumcised* enemy bringing reproach upon Israel. The importance of the word uncircumcised cannot be overstated. If the fight was between one faction or clan of Israel and another, the deal is off. But David knew from what was spewing out of his mouth that Goliath was not in covenant with David's God. Goliath would not have the mark of the covenant, circumcision, and instead would be uncovered and vulnerable no matter how much armor he wore.

We know the story from here, but look closer for the two things I mentioned earlier. What is God specifically, purposely, going to prove again? The people chose a man who was more handsome in a manly way and stronger in appearance because he was taller than his peers. There is a problem with that. No matter how impressively tall and strong you are, there will always be someone else coming along who is taller and stronger than you. This misplaced trust is exactly why the Philistines could put Israel in such an impossible situation.

Everyone in Israel is ignoring the 800-pound gorilla in the king's tent. The truth is, the reason for the taunt is that there is only one man in Israel who is literally head and shoulders taller than all the others. It is Saul. Saul is the one who *should* be answering the challenge and both sides know it. When their soldier who is head and shoulders taller and much stronger than Saul kills him, the Philistines will not just defeat another soldier. Goliath will kill the King of Israel and the nation will be theirs to plunder.

Israel, who is your choice? A man who is handsome in the way of a strong, mature, hardened warrior? Is it a man who is taller than all his peers, with a heavy and impressive helmet of bronze and a very heavy sword, who trusts in his own strength? Check.

Now God, who is Your choice? He is an adolescent, handsome in a ruddy looking (a youthful, red-faced) way. He is too small to even bear the weight of Saul's armor. God's choice will just rely on a slingshot, no helmet, sword, or shield. Oh, there is one more thing David has going for him. David knows to not trust in his appearance or his own strength.

David put his trust in his blood covenant with the God of Israel. Result? Game over.

> *Then said David to the Philistine, You come to me with a sword, a spear, and a javelin, but I come to you in the name of the Lord of hosts, the God of the ranks of Israel, Whom you have defied. This day the Lord will deliver you into my hand, and I will smite you and cut off your head. And I will give the corpses of the army of the Philistines this day to the birds of the air and the wild beasts of the earth, that all the earth may know that there is a God in Israel. And all this assembly shall know that the Lord saves not with sword and spear; for the battle is the Lord's, and He will give you into our hands.* (1 Samuel 17:45-47 AMPC)

A Blood Covenant at the High Noon of David's Life

What was David's Secret to his every success?

David was acknowledged by all to be faithful, strong, and brave. God continued to be with him in all his endeavors. At the high noon of his quickly developing stature and station in life, women were singing his praises in the streets.

✠

Yet, David continued to put his trust in the covenant-making God rather than in his own strength.

✠

David, because of his covenant oath to serve his country's king, continues to honor Saul even though Saul is not honoring his covenant and even attempting to kill David.

Jonathan was the son of King Saul and the next in line to inherit the Kingdom. The Bible tells us that although he still loved and wanted to believe the best of his father, Jonathan immediately accepted and loved David. It went beyond affection. Jonathan also approved of God's choice for who should be the next King of Israel, David. Apart from understanding covenant ceremonies, we may not realize that Jonathan is swearing to do more than just have affection for David. There needs to be a way for Jonathan to prove the depth of loyalty pledged to David. Jonathan would reveal this in the one way that would assure David of his knitted heart and the depth of his loyalty. Jonathan would ask David to cut a blood covenant.

> *Then Jonathan made a covenant with David, because he loved him as his own life. And Jonathan stripped himself of the robe that was on him and gave it to David, and his armor, even his sword, his bow, and his girdle.* (1 Samuel 17:45-47 AMPC)

Apart from understanding the mystery of blood covenants, you might not readily accept my assertion that Jonathan was doing more than just showing his affection for David.

We have already seen that important symbolic gifts are given during the covenant-making ceremony to demonstrate the length and depth of the impact that the covenant will have on their lives. We see only two details of their covenant ceremony recorded. The first is Jonathan's gift of all of his weapons. This means that Jonathan is pledging the use of all of his weapons to David, regardless of the enemy. This means that even if the attack planned on David comes from his own father, Jonathan is swearing to give his allegiance and protection to David. Jonathan's loyalty would be tested when, at his own peril, he confirmed David's suspicions of a plot to take David's life. Jonathan helped David escape the ambush his father arranged.

Let's unveil the covenant mystery and reveal the most important gift that Jonathan gave to David that day. Even to this day, when you see a person in uniform, it can tell you what branch of service, for what country, and at what level of authority the uniformed person is serving.

In Bible times, clothes made known the authority and station in life of the man even more so than they do today. Not just anyone could show up at the Temple, pretend to be blind or lame, and beg for alms. The Temple provided approved outer garments that confirmed the person's status as an authorized beggar. When a person who Jesus healed threw away his garment, he was throwing away his right to beg. It would no longer be needed. When the rich man's prodigal son came back home, among other things, the father had a robe placed upon him that signified he was now reinstated as the owner's son with full rights and authority restored.

Jonathan was identified as King Saul's son with all the rights and privileges of that rank and station in life by the outer garment he was wearing.[33] When he literally stripped himself of that robe and gave it to David, Jonathan was giving David his authority on and off the field of battle and his right to the throne.

A Blood-Covenant Story at the Twilight of David's Life

Saul was slain by an enemy, and unfortunately, Jonathan also lost his life in battle. Now, as the end of his story approaches, David has been the King of Israel for many years. It is nearing the sunset of his life and reign. Reflecting back on his life, David remembers his covenant with Jonathan. The covenant, as always, extends to heirs. David asks his people to find out if there is any blood relative of Jonathan that he can show kindness to because of his covenant with Jonathan.

---

[33] Strong's Dictionary. Strong's Number h4598.

Why we need to know who Mephibosheth is.

The men report back that there was a son of Jonathan hiding out on the backside of the desert in Lodebar. His father named him Mephibosheth. This shows the high hopes his father had for his son. He hoped his son would be following in his footsteps to fight valiantly on the side of the God of Israel. His name means *"Exterminator of the idol Baal,"* a chief god the Philistines worshipped. These hopes for the son were dashed the same day Jonathan died in battle. Now that David would be made king, the servants fled in terror. While doing so, the nurse caused him to have a fall that left him unable to walk for the rest of his life. He was not just limping; he was lame in both legs. That meant he was hopelessly and completely crippled.

The haste and hiding were not just out of concern for the enemies at the door. It was a common practice in that day, when a person not born of the prior king's household becomes king, to execute any legitimate bloodline heirs who could later challenge him for the throne.

Decades later, the servants of Saul's house, ostensibly loyal to David, still hold to the assumption that if David were to discover that a son of Jonathan remained alive, he would be executed. A direct lie to the king is punishable by death, so they tried not to answer. The first thing they told David was that the man he seeks was lame, hoping David would not pursue him further, given that the man was therefore not a threat. This does not deter David.

What the servants do not know is that covenant changes every-thing. Instead of exterminating the son of Jonathan as any normal king might do, David seeks to show him covenant *hessed* (mercy; lovingk-indness). This term is a covenant term that is hard to translate. The King James Version sometimes translates the word as mercy. It really means at one and the same time to give unmerited grace, favor, goodness, lov-ing-kindness, and tender mercy to one who does not, apart from cove-nant, deserve any such thing.

I am including this extending of covenant relationship to the son of Jonathan as one of the more important covenants to study because it unveils the *hessed*-based blood covenant. We know our covenant is also based on *hessed* because it provides us with unmerited grace, favor, goodness, loving-kindness, and tender mercy as ones who do not, apart from covenant, deserve any such thing.

Mephibosheth is required to come and bow what he is confident is his soon-to-be-severed head before the king.

> *And Mephibosheth son of Jonathan, the son of Saul, came to David and fell on his face and did obeisance. David said, Mephibosheth! And he answered, Behold your servant! David said to him, Fear not, for I will surely show you kindness [hessed] for Jonathan your father's sake, and will restore to you all the land of Saul your father [grandfather], and you shall eat at my table always. And [the cripple] bowed himself and said, What is your servant, that you should look upon such a dead dog as I am? Then the king called to Ziba, Saul's servant, and said to him, I have given your master's son [grandson] all that belonged to Saul and to all his house. And you shall till the land for him, you, your sons, and your servants, and you shall bring in the produce, that your master's heir may have food to eat; but Mephibosheth, your master's son [grandson], shall eat always at my table.* (2 Samuel 9:6-10 AMPC)

There is a common thread throughout the story. Once he became lame, Mephibosheth for all intents and purposes was alive, but as good as dead. He could have no chance of soldiering aside his father, ruling or reigning, or even being accepted as a whole man. People were looking for an imposing figure to be their figurehead. He was a cripple and was perceived as having no worth. He thinks now that his grandfather having been king, instead of a blessing, has become the final curse that would end his wretched life. In his own mind, he was as worthless as a dead dog.

> *So Mephibosheth dwelt in Jerusalem, for he ate continually at the king's table, [even though] he was lame in both feet.* (2 Samuel 9:13 AMPC)

The heritage Mephibosheth feared was the source of his salvation. As a son of the covenant maker, he received all the blessings, benefits, station in life, land, and possessions of his father and his father's father. David is saying, "You did not earn it, you cannot do anything to repay, and you do not deserve it. All that would have been yours if you and/or your ancestors had not fallen, is forfeited, it is mine. But because of my covenant with your father, I am giving all of it to you. I will treat you as if you never fell. I will treat you as one of my own sons, including a seat at my table. You may be helpless in your own strength, but I will give you my authority, and all of your father's servants, to help you possess and benefit from your inheritance."

Our inheritance, hidden in the mystery of the blood covenants, is herein revealed. Jesus is saying to us, "You did not earn it, you cannot do anything to repay, and you do not deserve it. All that would have been yours if you and/or your ancestors had not fallen, is Mine. But, because of My covenant with your Father, I am giving all of it to you. I will treat you as if you never fell. I will treat you as one of My own sons, including a seat at My table. You may be helpless in your own strength, but I will give you My authority, and all of your Father's ministering angels, to help you possess and benefit from your inheritance."

Blood Covenant as seen in David's Psalm 23

The template for the covenant blessings that David provided to the son of Jonathan was a *hessed*-based blood covenant. God revealed by His

Spirit to David that this was the basis for their own relationship. David's understanding of *hessed* is seen in his Psalm 23.

> *THE LORD is my Shepherd [to feed, guide, and shield me], I shall not lack. He makes me lie down in [fresh, tender] green pastures; He leads me beside the still and restful waters. He refreshes and restores my life (my self); He leads me in the paths of righteousness [uprightness and right standing with Him—not for my earning it, but] for His name's sake. Yes, though I walk through the [deep, sunless] valley of the shadow of death, I will fear or dread no evil, for You are with me; Your rod [to protect] and Your staff [to guide], they comfort me. You prepare a table before me in the presence of my enemies. You anoint my head with oil; my [brimming] cup runs over. Surely or only goodness, mercy, and unfailing love shall follow me all the days of my life, and through the length of my days the house of the Lord [and His presence] shall be my dwelling place.* (Psalm 23:1-6 AMPC)

Now, let's take everything we are learning about blood covenants and apply it to our reading. We will see that David is telling us a whole lot more about our *hessed* covenant than you might otherwise glean from its poetic verses.

The Lord is my Shepherd [to feed, guide, and shield me], I shall not lack.

> *A Lord is the covenant leader who has taken an oath to provide for and protect those he leads; a flock of sheep-shepherd, a family-patriarch, a medieval province-Lord of that realm, a nation-king, a creation-Creator God, the Kingdom of God-Jesus. Because of your blood covenant*

with Jesus, you will not lack anything; He will feed, guide, and shield you.

He makes me lie down in [fresh, tender] green pastures; He leads me beside the still and restful waters.

Jesus provides all you have need of, all that pertains to sustaining the life needs of this physical body. Jesus will demonstrate this in Matthew 14:19 when He commands His flock of followers to lie down in the fresh tender green grass beside the water of Lake Galilee where He feeds them.

He refreshes and restores my life (my self).

We also have needs of the heart and spirit. Jesus provides all that pertains to life, as a free gift. He also provides all that pertains to godliness as a free gift; being spiritually prosperous, enjoying peace, joy, love, forgiveness, and experiencing the favor of God.

He leads me in the paths of righteousness [uprightness and right standing with Him—not for my earning it, but] for His name's sake.

The additional clarity provided by the AMPC version of this Psalm alone is worth finding a copy and reading it when you want to study the Bible.[34] Clearly, we see that the leading in righteous paths is not earned or a byproduct of our own good works qualifying us to be placed on that path. It is the byproduct of having been placed in His blood covenant and thereby given His name, as a bride

---

[34] AMPC is available to read for free on Bible.com.

benefits from all that her spouse has, by taking on the name of the husband in a blood covenant of marriage.

Yes, though I walk through the [deep, sunless] valley of the shadow of death, I will fear or dread no evil, for You are with me; Your rod [to protect] and Your staff [to guide], they comfort me.

God's path is the righteous path, where it is never sunless and there is no shadow of death. David knew that you should stay on the son-lit path, out of this valley. But valleys happen. Sometimes, you are sent there to rescue a lamb. Sometimes, you get there all to your own discredit, and now you are the lamb in need of rescue. David stumbled into dark valleys more than once. The important thing he knew, because of his covenant, was that God was the same kind of shepherd to him, that he was to his sheep.

There are other scriptures where you can draw a sermon up about how a good father does not spare the rod. This is not one of them. David, and God, never used the tool intended for the protection of the sheep to harm the sheep. He used the rod on the animals attacking the sheep, not on the sheep, "Your rod to protect." If you fear what is in the hand of the shepherd, you will not allow him to draw near for protection or to guide you with the staff. There is therefore now no condemnation (no beating the sheep to teach them a lesson) done by the hand of Jesus), not to those now in His name, in hessed-covenant with Jesus.[35]

---

[35] Romans 8:1

You prepare a table before me in the presence of my enemies. You anoint my head with oil; my [brimming] cup runs over.

> *I have often heard Psalm 23 at memorial services and I would not object if it were made part of one for me. But did you notice that this banquet table, this anointing oil, this cup of blessing brimming over, are provided in the presence of my enemies? My enemies are not in heaven. I will not need the relief from the heat provided by being anointed with oil in heaven. David had enemies and divine triumph over them in the days of his life, not after it. All of these covenant blessings and all of this provision is to minister to my needs on this side of the river. They will not be required in the sweet by and by, they are needed right here, in the ugly here and now.*

Surely or only goodness, mercy, and unfailing love [hessed] shall follow me all the days of my life.

> *Here again, note the context is speaking of the here and now, not the afterlife. Hessed will attend my steps during all the days of my life. As explained before, this one little word hessed packs quite a punch. It is a covenant term and embodies many specific covenant blessings promised to those who are in Christ. And it is here and now that I need hessed; goodness, mercy, favor, physical and spiritual blessings, unfailing love, loving-kindness, and tender mercies.*

And through the length of my days the house of the Lord [and His presence] shall be my dwelling place.

There is no timeframe to this verse except for when it begins. It begins the day you accept Jesus as the one who died for your sins. His death did more than just pay for your sins, His blood ratified the new and better covenant you now have with the Father, Son, and Holy Spirit. It is the basis of your new relationship with Father God through Jesus Christ. You become one with Jesus, and you are by covenant decree identified now as a son of God.

This being in "the house of the Lord" starts now and endures for eternity. You are to be dwelling in the House of the Lord in two ways, not one. Yes, He did go and prepare a place for us to dwell after this life. If you pass from this life before His return, you will be immediately absent from this life, and present with Him where He is now. But when Jesus leaves where He is now and comes back here, you will be here with Him. When the new heavens and earth arrive, you will be there with Him. This is because you are not just going to one day be in a physical housing project He prepared. Wherever He is, you will be also.

The House of the Lord also refers to your being adopted into His household. If you are a descendent of the Tudor family, you are long lost royalty. You are of the House of Tudor. If you are in Christ, you are grafted into the royal family tree of the anointed and His anointing. I was previously only of the House of Donaldson. Now I am also of the House of God. Human dynasties come and go, but being a part of the Family of God has benefits now, and the retirement benefits are out of this world.

Key Points: Review and Reflect

Morning of David's Life:

What was the secret to David's every success?

Why did being a head taller than all of Israel become both a blessing and a curse to King Saul?

What was promised to the man of Israel who defeated Goliath?

Did David get all of them in spite of King Saul's spite?

High Noon of David's Life:

What was the significance of the covenant gifts Jonathan gave to David?

Did David receive what they promised?

Twilight of David's Life:

Why do we need to know who Mephibosheth is?

How did other people see him and why?

How did he see himself and why?

How did King David see him?

What is a *hessed*-based blood covenant?

Psalm 23

What does it mean to dwell in the House of the Lord?

Continue to record in your journal how the impact of what you are learning is affecting your life.

Proclaiming the Arrival of the New and Better Covenant

Why is the "Sermon on the Mount" not a sermon?

As I begin to write each new chapter, my heart is full of expectation and excitement. I have such a passion to share what I have learned because of how it has changed my life for the better in every conceivable way. I sincerely begin to write each chapter believing it is the most important one in the book. I feel this way again, more than ever. Why? It is because we have come so far, and it has all led to this, being able to proclaim the arrival of the long-awaited New and Better Covenant. All of the blood covenants which preceded this one were instructive. We would not have what we have without them. Yet this repurposed phrase from Star Wars comes to mind, "These are not the covenants you are looking for."

This is the covenant you are looking for. This is the one that was promised, hoped for, and sought after for hundreds of years. Yet, they did not see it coming when it finally came. We have to remember that in part, this is because its fulfillment had to be veiled from the prying eyes of those religious leaders whose hearts were as cold as stone, and from the enemy of our souls.

But we speak the wisdom of God in a mystery, the hidden wisdom which God ordained before the ages for our glory, which none of the rulers of this age knew; for had they known, they would not have crucified the Lord of glory.
(1 Corinthians 2:7-8 NKJV)

Veiled to those who were there, and to others yet today, we must see this announcement at His appearing in light of the unveiled mystery of the blood covenant—to hear and see what others have missed.

Proclaiming the Arrival to Shepherds on the Hillsides

*But the angel said to them, Do not be afraid; for behold, I bring you **good news** of a great joy which will come to all the people. For to you is born this day in the town of David a Savior, Who is Christ (the **Messiah**) the Lord!*
(Luke 2:10-11 emphasis added)

The first to hear the Good News after Jesus was physically born of a woman into the earth were shepherds. The reason it was revealed to them by the angelic host is because the new and better covenant would be sealed by the blood of a sacrificial lamb. This lamb must meet the requirements of the perfect, unblemished sheep suitable for use as a sacrifice offered at the Temple on the Day of Atonement. On that day, lambs would become a covenant sacrifice to take away the sins of Israel for another year. The same shepherds who were raising lambs that met the stringent requirements to be acceptable for that sacrifice were asked to come and inspect the Lamb of God. They were sent to the place of His birth to confirm that He met with their approval. Jesus was placed in the one place in Bethlehem where a number of shepherds would have been allowed to enter, in the middle of the night, a stable. There they observed the Lamb of God and praised God for Him.

Proclaiming the Arrival to Keepers of the Law in Their Synagogues

Those who attended Sabbath ceremonies at their synagogue should have been the first to receive Him once the grown Jesus began His public ministry. They revered and studied the scriptures religiously and tried to keep the laws of the Mosaic Covenant.

More than four hundred years prior to Jesus taking on human flesh, Isaiah prophesied to Israel that the Messiah would be sent to them and would proclaim the Good News upon His arrival. Isaiah included many specific covenant blessings that would accompany the Messiah. The coming Covenant leader, Messiah, King, would heal the physically hurting, heal the spiritually hurting, free the captives and slaves to sin, and deliver righteousness to those who yearn for it.

> *THE SPIRIT of the Lord God is upon me, because the Lord has anointed and qualified me to preach the Gospel of good tidings to the meek, the poor, and afflicted; He has sent me to bind up and heal the brokenhearted, to proclaim liberty to the [physical and spiritual] captives and the opening of the prison and of the eyes to those who are bound, to proclaim the acceptable year of the Lord [the year of His favor] and the day of vengeance of our God, to comfort all who mourn, to grant [consolation and joy] to those who mourn in Zion—to give them an ornament (a garland or diadem) of beauty instead of ashes, the oil of joy instead of mourning, the garment [expressive] of praise instead of a heavy, burdened, and failing spirit— that they may be called oaks of righteousness [lofty, strong, and magnificent, distinguished for uprightness, justice, and right standing with God], the planting of the Lord, that He may be glorified. (Isaiah 61:1-3 AMPC)*

Jesus read these verses from Isaiah to the congregation assembled in the synagogue. His audience was very familiar with the passages and likely could have recited them from heart. Reading these passages out of the scroll of the book of Isaiah was not unusual, but what Jesus said next shocked them to the core of their being. He said, "Today, this Scripture has been fulfilled while you are present and hearing."

> *The Spirit of the Lord [is] upon Me, because He has anointed Me [the Anointed One, the Messiah] to preach the good news (the Gospel) to the poor; He has sent Me to announce release to the captives and recovery of sight to the blind, to send forth as delivered those who are oppressed [who are downtrodden, bruised, crushed, and broken down by calamity], to proclaim the accepted and acceptable year of the Lord [the day when salvation and the free favors of God profusely abound].* (Luke 4:18-19 AMPC)

Easily, this was the best message ever spoken to a congregation, but it was not well received. You might say His ministry got off to a bit of a rocky start when some picked up stones and others tried to drive Him off a cliff.

Proclaiming the Arrival to All with Ears to Hear on the Mountainsides

After attempted murder became the routine response of the majority of the churchgoers of His day, Jesus took His core message to those outside the walls of the church. He crisscrosses the nation of Israel for three years proclaiming, and then doing the same things He said He would do in Luke 4:18. Jesus now proclaims the arrival of the Messiah and the blessings that accompany His appearing on the mountainsides across Israel. This is the genesis of the full-blown, out there, hear ye, hear ye, proclamation to all the world recorded for us in Matthew 5.

This is why I believe the title added to these verses much later by some editors that called it a "sermon" on the mount, is at best, lackluster. This is no sermon telling listeners to endure their hardships with a stiff upper lip. Jesus is not telling them to live a meek, humble, and moral life. This is a proclamation of freedom for anyone being oppressed, downtrodden, bruised, crushed, or broken down by calamity. I propose that a more correct title for His message in Matthew 5 would be:

"The Proclamation of the New Blood Covenant Blessings on the Mount"

Jesus was spelling out what came with the acceptance of Him as their Messiah, their Covenant Head, their King, and His Kingdom of Heaven. In the synagogue, Jesus proclaimed that He is the Messiah who was to bring the covenant promises of deliverance with Him when He came. Now, Jesus was out on the mountainside doing it. From this venue, all in Israel would be able to hear Him proclaim, "I am anointed and qualified to preach the Gospel of good tidings to the meek, the poor, and afflicted; God has sent me to bind up and heal the brokenhearted, to proclaim liberty to the [physical and spiritual] captives and the opening of the prison and of the eyes to those who are blind."

The word used at the beginning of the following verses is a very strong and purposely chosen word, *blessed*. It means happy, enviably fortunate, and filled to overflowing with joy. Yet, many in His audience were meek, poor, and afflicted. Some were brokenhearted and spiritually impoverished. Others were feeling the effects of sin while striving for unattainable levels of righteousness.

These are not good conditions to be in or attitudes to adopt. They are bad conditions that Jesus abhors. They are conditions that are the byproducts of sin for which there was no cure until the advent of the Messiah.

Jesus is telling them the Good News, which is, their Messiah has come, their deliverer is going to now bless them with deliverance from any and all of these afflictions. Furthermore, He is not just going to tell them that someday they will be blessed, He is actually going to heal the sick and more. He is giving them, and you and me, the opportunity to accept Him as Messiah, Savior, and Covenant King.

We can all be translated into the Kingdom of Heaven while still alive and on this earth. We do not have to die and be raised from the grave to inherit the promises, but Jesus would have to die and be raised from the dead to deliver these promises to us.

Here is my covenant unveiling commentary on the Proclamation of Blood Covenant Blessings on the Mount, found in Matthew 5:1-10 line by line.

1 And seeing the multitudes, He went up into a mountain: and when He was set, His disciples came unto Him:

- This message in Matthew is for all who followed Him out to this mountain to hear it. Luke will tell of another mountain, another location, another assembled group, but it will be the same message and the same results everywhere He went.

2 And He opened His mouth, and taught them, saying,

- In Genesis, Jesus spoke, and creation happened. Jesus will now use His words to speak forth the fulfillment of the promised Messiah coming. Jesus proclaiming these blessings, speaking them into the earth, caused healing and deliverance to be the signs that would follow and accompany His Word.

3 Blessed are the poor in spirit: for theirs is the kingdom of heaven.

- Jesus is saying to those whose sense of spiritual worth is impoverished; you are blessed, enviably happy, because I am giving you all the spiritual wealth reserved for the righteous citizens of my Kingdom. John was the most spiritually great of all men in the old covenant, but the least in My Kingdom, My new and better covenant is greater than he.[36]

4 Blessed are they that mourn: for they shall be comforted.

- The context of the phrase *"Those who mourn,"* is the verse in Isaiah 61:3 which Jesus is fulfilling. They are mourning the crushing loss of their nation Israel and its capital city, Jerusalem, to the cruel rule of heathen nations. Jesus proclaims deliverance from mourning, promising that they will be comforted. They will be comforted in two ways. They can choose to receive entrance into the greater Kingdom they are being offered with comfort and joy that exceeds any blessing born of restored national pride in an earthly kingdom. There will also one day be a redemption of the physical kingdom of the nation of Israel at His yet to be revealed future appearing.

5 Blessed are the meek: for they shall inherit the earth.

- Cease and desist from ever equating "meek" and "humble" in these verses with being laudably humble, lowly, and gentle. In Isaiah 61:1, the Hebrew word for meek is *Anayv*: it means depressed, humbled by wretched circumstances, lowly, poor, weak, and afflicted. In the New Testament, the word is *praus*: humble and longsuffering. The Greek term can have two meanings, easily determined by the context of the verse it appears in. In Matthew 11:11, meek is used speaking of Jesus when He describes Himself as a meek, humble, and longsuffering taskmaster; rather than an overbearing, demanding, and harsh taskmaster. In that context, meekness is laudable because it is a conscious choice of someone who has the authority and power to choose His attitude.

  In Isaiah 61:1, the meekness and humbleness are not by choice. They are the condition of a helpless weakened slave being beaten for no reason by an overbearing taskmaster, just the opposite

---

[36] Matthew 11:11

of Jesus. Seen in that context, one should feel righteous anger for the sufferer and the condition of his impoverished spirit in Matthew 5:5. Meekness here is the meekness of one being literally beaten into submission and helpless. The good news that is making the meek and humble rejoice in this verse is not that they have learned to accept their torment humbly or learned humility through their suffering. The good news Jesus delivered is that they are going to inherit the earth alongside Jesus. They will be the owners, not the owned. They will rule justly in this life as meek (in the good sense) taskmasters, and noble kings.[37]

6 Blessed are they which do hunger and thirst after righteousness: for they shall be filled.

- What is the problem here that the deliverer is going to resolve? These sufferers feel the pain of their spiritual condition worse than others might feel physical hunger. The problem is that they cannot ever achieve the level of righteousness that a holy God requires, as is the case with all mankind being affected by Adam's inherited spiritual death. The good news is that what they could never work hard enough to obtain is now being given to them as a free gift. It is only by New Blood Covenant grace that redemption from their particular plight can be delivered to them. It is important to see that the blessedness comes, not from their striving to be good, but from the gift of righteousness being given to them.

7 Blessed are the merciful: for they shall obtain mercy.

- Being merciful is certainly a good trait to have; I would not argue otherwise. The problem is that more often than not, being merciful in a dark and sin-ridden world does not result in receiving mercy in return. In nations that do not incorporate Judeo-Christian ethics in their culture, being merciful is

---

[37] Romans 5:17

often considered a sign of weakness. You might receive mercy, you might not. Jesus is pleased to be able to say, "Good news merciful ones, your Messiah deliverer has added mercy to the inherited promises of the New Covenant." Unlimited, unmerited, and tender mercy is obtained by whosoever accepts the covenant Jesus is proclaiming to be theirs for the asking.

8 Blessed are the pure in heart: for they shall see God.

- This promised blessing is a corollary to the one in verse 6. Both followers are exhibiting a good trait, as best they can. The word for pure here is used to denote one being ceremonially clean by following the Mosaic Covenant religious rituals and dietary laws. By adding the word *heart* to the word *pure* in this passage, Jesus is kicking it up a notch. Some may hone a talent for showing their cleanliness by outward appearances, but the truly pure must nail the harder task, to be pure in heart. Later in His message, Jesus explains that refraining from physical adultery with the body is not good enough. If you only have unclean thoughts that you never acted on, you fail the test of perfect righteousness.

  By the way, Jesus did not raise this issue to get them to try harder, it was to compel them to give up trying to attempt to earn what it is not possible in your own strength to obtain. The offered benefit to those striving to be pure in heart is brilliant. From the implementation of Mosaic Law forward, the unclean know that they cannot look upon God and live. This level of perfection is simply not possible for fallen man. The Good News for them is that the believer who desires to be pure inside and out will be given a clean heart as a gift, they can now see God and live. When they accept His offer, their spiritual eyes will be opened and they will realize that if they have seen Jesus, they have in fact, already seen God.

9 Blessed are the peacemakers: for they shall be called the children of God.

- Peacemaker is an interesting Greek contraction of the words for *peace* and *maker of.* The contraction only appears this one time in scripture, while its root word peace appears more than ninety times. While it is laudable to be one who seeks peace between nations and with others, this verse's promise is directly related to the benefit they will be getting when they accept the kind of peace that the Messiah is offering to them. When they accept the blood covenant, they become heirs of that covenant. God is now their Father God; they are adopted into His family. You shall be called the children of God. Only the peace of rec-onciliation brought by accepting the New Covenant will make it possible for earthly peacemakers to be called the children of God. While being peacemakers is laudable, it is very important to realize that their good works are not what Jesus is praising or is the basis for being called the children of God. I hope this is becoming clear.

  In every instance, the blessed are receiving a source of unspeak-able joy because they are being delivered from a situation they could not otherwise escape. In every instance, it is not their works or their endurance of hardship or their laudable attitude that causes their release or their happiness.

  These peacemakers are being reached out to with the Good News that will benefit them in a way that far exceeds any ben-efit from brokering peace among men. The peacemakers will not get one inch closer to peace with God by their works. They will be rewarded with adoption and have eternal peace with God by accepting the Messiah who is offering them a greater peace than they could otherwise achieve.

10 Blessed are they which are persecuted for righteousness' sake: for theirs is the kingdom of heaven. (Matthew 5:1-10 KJV)

- Some find themselves reaping the result of their misdeeds. They have earned their persecution and prosecution. Others are persecuted when they have done no wrong. This was a constant occurrence under Roman rule and any regime where corrupt political figures turn the power of the state against their own people. A perfect modern example is the persecution of Jews under the Nazi regime and the horror of the holocaust. Imagine what it was like to be a people who were good upstanding citizens, had a religious compulsion to do well, obeyed the laws, and lived by a strict code of moral conduct. Yet, they found themselves helpless victims of those with a demonically inspired hatred of the righteous. Trainloads of victims were sentenced to death camps for the crime of being Jewish.

These are some of those whose meekness is forced upon them by a merciless taskmaster. See yourself standing with me beside the liberating forces just outside the tall barbed-wire fences. We are looking through the fence at emaciated men in their filthy striped prisoner uniforms.

The commanding officer proclaims, "Gentlemen, your days of unjust persecution are over. Your captivity is immediately ended this day. Though you were forced into the meekness and humbleness of the captive by merciless tools of the kingdom of darkness, you are now being led out of captivity and into the protection of the Allied Forces. Your stolen homes and looted businesses will be returned to you. Your stolen art treasures, as soon as we find them, will be returned to you. Your citizenship and right standing in your nation will be restored to you."

The Good News for you and me today, for all who can identify with any of the groups included by Jesus in His proclamation, is this. We can have more than just our physical needs met, we can have our spiritual needs met, also—covenant bread for the body and covenant fruit of the Vine for the spirit. We can enjoy every kind of deliverance Jesus proclaimed as our covenant rights and privileges in the Kingdom of Heaven. That Kingdom for us has come and His will is being done on earth, as it is in Heaven.

We need to hear this Good News to develop our faith in His provision of covenant grace, covenant faith, and covenant favor. Fortunately, this is exactly what is on deck for the next three chapters.

Before we leave the book of Matthew, consider the Amplified Classic Version's translation of these verses. Blessed, *makarios,* is a word purposely chosen by the inspired writer of the original text for its being a poetic, prolonged form of the root word blessed. The full impact of these verses deserves and is revealed by this version's amplified treatment of the word *makarios.*

The Proclamation of Covenant Blessings – Amplified.

1 SEEING THE crowds, He went up on the mountain; and when He was seated, His disciples came to Him.

2 Then He opened His mouth and taught them, saying:

3 Blessed (happy, to be envied, and spiritually prosperous—with life-joy and satisfaction in God's favor and salvation, regardless of their outward conditions) are the poor in spirit (the humble, who rate themselves insignificant), for theirs is the kingdom of heaven!

4 Blessed and enviably happy [with a happiness produced by the experience of God's favor and especially conditioned by the revelation of His matchless grace] are those who mourn, for they shall be comforted!

5 Blessed (happy, blithesome, joyous, spiritually prosperous—with life-joy and satisfaction in God's favor and salvation, regardless of their outward conditions) are the meek (the mild, patient, long-suffering), for they shall inherit the earth!

6 Blessed and fortunate and happy and spiritually prosperous (in that state in which the born-again child of God enjoys His favor and salvation) are those who hunger and thirst for righteousness (uprightness and right standing with God), for they shall be completely satisfied!

7 Blessed (happy, to be envied, and spiritually prosperous—with life-joy and satisfaction in God's favor and salvation, regardless of their outward conditions) are the merciful, for they shall obtain mercy!

8 Blessed (happy, enviably fortunate, and spiritually prosperous—possessing the happiness produced by the experience of God's favor and especially conditioned by the revelation of His grace, regardless of their outward conditions) are the pure in heart, for they shall see God!

9 Blessed (enjoying enviable happiness, spiritually prosperous—with life-joy and satisfaction in God's favor and salvation, regardless of their outward conditions) are the makers and maintainers of peace, for they shall be called the sons of God!

10 Blessed and happy and enviably fortunate and spiritually prosperous (in the state in which the born-again child of God enjoys and finds satisfaction in God's favor and salvation, regardless of his outward conditions) are those who are persecuted for righteousness' sake (for being and doing right), for theirs is the kingdom of heaven! (Matthew 5:1-10 AMPC)

Why is the word "sermon" an inadequate title for what is presented in Matthew's verses that begin with the word "blessed?"

THE SPIRIT of the Lord God is upon me, because the Lord has anointed and qualified me to preach the Gospel of good tidings to the meek, the poor, and afflicted; He has sent me to bind up and heal the brokenhearted, to proclaim liberty to the [physical and spiritual] captives and the opening of the prison and of the eyes to those who are bound. (Isaiah 61:1)

How does Isaiah 61:1 help us understand what Jesus is proclaiming, not sermonizing about, on the mount?

In your own words, what would be a better name for the passages labeled "The Sermon on the Mount?"

Which of the eight groups of people in these passages do you most closely identify with as being in a condition you have experienced?

Being or having been in that condition, would you find the deliverance Jesus promises to those who accept Him to be good news?

If you have accepted Jesus as your Covenant King and received the gift of being made by faith pure in heart, what accompanies you now being able to see God? (Hint: *makarios*)

Who do you know that needs to hear this covenant-infused commentary on the first ten verses of Matthew 5? Will you share it with them?

Write down the results you get from sharing this message. (Heartfelt thanks or rock throwing?)

Continue to record in your journal how the impact of what you are learning is affecting your life.

-8-

Enjoying Covenant Grace

✠

Do you realize that only the right understanding of Blood Covenant can convey to you the mindset God was just dying to give you?

Unveiling the Secret to Enjoying Covenant Grace

There are more than a dozen churches in close proximity to me whose name contains the word "grace." There are Grace Point, Grace Lutheran. Grace United Methodist, Grace Baptist, Grace Presbyterian, Our Lady of Grace, and more. Their Statements of Faith are as diverse as Baptist is from Catholic. All lay claim to being a place where someone who wants to go to a church known for "grace" would feel welcome.

Do you suppose grace may mean different things to different people?

Many secular businesses incorporate *grace* into their names from hospitals to hair salons, a photography studio, the home of the King of Rock and Roll, and a coffee vendor on a college campus. They are very clever choices, even if it happens to just be the first name of a family member. You want your hospitals to be gracious in how they treat you. You want your stylist to grace your locks with beauty. You want your photographs to evoke grace and style in how they make you look. Graceland, for me, evokes thoughts of Elvis' love of Gospel music. But his home was actually named that by the first owners, Dr. and Mrs. Thomas Moore, after the wife's aunt. I am not sure what inspired someone to call their business Grace Coffee Company, but it does make me want to try some.

Grace is more than just a word with a nice connotation that might entice customers to your location. Some of the grace-named churches above would say if you ask Him, Jesus will forgive your sins with His "saving grace." The better news is that unveiling the secret of "blood covenant grace" can transform your relationship from one where you are well aware of your sins and relieved to be a forgiven sinner, to what it really means to be a new creation—a wholly righteous born anew child of God. You can be enjoying all that we saw in the preceding chapter Jesus proclaimed to be yours. **The revelation of His grace** is vital to obtaining the full dimensions of the relationship and its blessings that Matthew 5:8 tells us are ours.

> *Blessed (happy, enviably fortunate, and spiritually prosperous—possessing the happiness produced by the experience of God's favor and **especially conditioned by the revelation of His grace**, regardless of their outward conditions) are the pure in heart, for they shall see God!* (AMPC emphasis added).

When we studied this scripture in the last chapter, we saw that accepting Jesus as your Blood Covenant Lord is the one and only way to become truly, perfectly, pure in heart. This purity is part of what the blood covenant relationship provides as a gift, not as a reward for behavior. When you ask Jesus to be your Savior, whether you realize it or not, you are asking Him to be your Messiah-Savior, your Covenant

Lord. The blood covenant is the basis for the saving relationship. Blood-covenant grace is the basis for the offer of the blood covenant.

When you accept the New and Better Covenant offered by Jesus, you will be held by Father God as being sinless. This qualifies you to be able to see God just as He promised. You now see, with the eyes of your heart, the triune Father God, Son Jesus, and Holy Spirit.

The acceptance of the offered covenant also qualifies you to receive all of the other blessings the above verse proclaims are given to you. These blessings include being happy, enviably fortunate, and spiritually prosperous—possessing the happiness produced by the experience of God's favor.

But notice, there is a catch!

Are these blessings limited in any way by your circumstances, your position in life, or your outward conditions? No. The verse says all of this is yours, regardless of outward conditions. Has your experiencing of the aforementioned blessings been a quart shy of a full gallon? What then, if anything, is the limiting factor? The answer is why I wrote this chapter. Matthew 5:8 clearly says the degree, the amount of being happy, enviably fortunate, spiritually prosperous, and possessing the happiness produced by the experience of God's favor are **especially conditioned by the revelation of His grace.**

✠

**We need a greater revelation of His grace
to understand and enjoy all that grace provides.**

✠

I love one of the most well-known songs in Christendom, *Amazing Grace*. As great as the saving grace referenced in that song is, grace is actually far more amazing than those lyrics convey. The Greek word used in the original text of the New Testament is *charis.*[38] Are you ready for this? Being given grace means to receive acceptable benefits and the ability to benefit from being deemed acceptable. It also means to be given unmerited favor, and that which affords joy, pleasure, delight, sweetness, loveliness; all of which are also unmerited gifts. The definition goes even further. Grace is included in what you can expect from someone showing *hessed*, a covenant term for the receiving of loving-kindness and tender mercy. If that were not enough, to be given grace also means to be given strength and an increased ability to do what one has been "graced" to be able to do. There are gifts of the Holy Spirit given to mankind to increase the ability to minister spiritually to those in need. The word for gifts in that familiar passage is *charismata*, coming from the same root word for grace.

This is a lot to absorb. Just take a moment to consider what it means to now have the revelation of a covenant grace-infused life.

- You are given acceptable benefits and the ability to benefit from being deemed acceptable.

- You have a source of great favor.

- You have a source of what affords joy, pleasure, delight, sweetness, loveliness; all of which is unmerited.

- This Grace is given to you out of *hessed*, which we know is a covenant term for bestowing loving kindness and tender mercy.

- Covenant grace provides power and enablement by way of spiritual gifts.

- Grace equips you as the scripture says, to be able to do all things in Christ.[39]

Unveiling the covenant grace basis of your relationship with Jesus and Father God can change your life. You have a God-given covenant

---

[38] Strong's Concordance Dictionary.

[39] Philippians 4:13

right to experience not only forgiveness, but also righteousness, peace, joy, and life more abundantly.

✠

God would have to break His Covenant promises *not* to give you what He has promised to you by grace, through faith.

✠

Since faith is involved and works like a seed, it is imperative to get this word, this seed, firmly planted and watered. Our confidence in what we believe must come from the Bible, not from our own experience or persuasive motivational messages. I deeply regret that for decades I was either opposed to or ignorant of almost everything that I am telling you about blood covenants. I was "born again" at an early age, but without the benefit of understanding my relationship with God was based upon blood-covenant promises and principles.

Previously, I shared how I was confronted with a cassette tape about the blood covenant after graduating from a highly accredited Christian College at the top of my class. I was fully prepared to completely refute the covenant blood teaching I was not familiar with by looking at the referenced Bible verses. It was reading these scriptures with new-covenant awareness that changed my life. I had to either cling to the old beliefs or accept the truth of the Word, whether it lined up with my experience or not. I am so thankful that I gave the Holy Spirit an opportunity to reveal this truth hidden in plain sight in the scriptures.

The verses the Holy Spirit has the potential to make come alive to us regarding covenant grace, faith, and favor have always been there. However, apart from unveiling blood-covenant truth, we might see without seeing and hear without hearing.

The Book of Romans and the other letters to churches are written looking back at the finished work of Jesus depicted in the Gospels after the Holy Spirit opened their spiritual eyes to see and ears to hear. The letters were written to the church with the help of the Holy Spirit to reveal the Good News of a New and Better Covenant being offered to all men.

> *For if by one man's offence death reigned by one; much more they which receive abundance of grace and of the gift of righteousness shall reign in life by one, Jesus Christ. Therefore as by the offence of one judgment came upon all men to condemnation; even so by the righteousness of one the free gift came upon all men unto justification of life. For as by one man's disobedience many were made sinners, so by the obedience of one shall many be made righteous.* (Romans 5:17-18 KJV)

This KJV text may be familiar, but not as easily and fully understood as it would be if presented in plain, modern, English. It was a breakthrough that cannot be overstated for us to benefit from the work of Martin Luther and those who soon followed his lead, to translate the Bible into our native tongues for us. I am fond of the King James Version; it is lovely, poetic, and I grew up on it. However, after four hundred years or so, many of us in the English-speaking former colonies have lost a knack for comprehending the archaic English of the King James Bible.

I like to teach from the Amplified Classic version because it is in today's English. Its focus is on accuracy as it pertains to faithfully representing Greek and Hebrew text original works in the English language. It is not in any way a modern paraphrase. The AMPC is willing to sacrifice brevity for a more precise and accurate rendering of the original Greek words. It is not adding text that was not there, it is adding text where one single English word does not adequately convey the thought that would have been fully understood by one fluent in Greek. I take the time to mention this because understanding the message directly from scripture is most important. I do not want you troubled by this more extensive and accurate treatment differing from the revered KJV.

For if because of one man's trespass (lapse, offense) death reigned through that one, much more surely will those who receive [God's] overflowing grace (unmerited favor) and the free gift of righteousness [putting them into right standing with Himself] reign as kings in life through the one Man Jesus Christ (the Messiah, the Anointed One). Well then, as one man's trespass [one man's false step and falling away led] to condemnation for all men, so one Man's act of righteousness [leads] to acquittal and right standing with God and life for all men. (Romans 5:17-18 AMPC)

Without further explanation, you can see that these verses are telling us that grace and righteousness, leading to acquittal and right standing with God, are being made available through something that Jesus Christ did. These verses are chockfull of covenant terminology, so let's break it down further so that with covenant vision, you can fully understand what is being revealed here.

For if because of one man's trespass (lapse, offense) death reigned through that one...

- The one man's trespass was Adam's. As long as he honored his covenant, Adam reigned in life, having been given authority over all creation. His covenant-breaking offense was to elevate the word of Satan over the word of God. Contrary to what God said, Adam believed Satan's lie that disobedience would not result in his death, but instead, make him more like God. As Dr. Phil says, "How is that working out for you?"

- Half-truths can be deadly. Breaking covenant did make Adam more like God in knowing about evil. At the same time, it made him less like God by now having to experience calamity and death personally. The result is that all mankind was made subject to death and dying; death reigned.

Much more surely will those who receive [God's] overflowing grace (unmerited favor) and the free gift of righteousness [putting them into right standing with Himself]...

- We are being told that what we are about to read is much more reliable, certain, and sure, than death. What is surer than death? A blood covenant-based oath of God is more sure and certain than death. This is why Abraham accepted God's blood covenant oath as the final word on whether or not he would have sons from Isaac, even if Isaac were to die by Abraham's own hand. God's blood covenant oath is what gave Abraham the confidence that God would raise the child from the dead, they would go back home together, and children would come forth from Isaac.

- Those who come to know and accept the covenant relationship and promises in this verse can be confident because God does not break His Covenant Word. What was promised?

    - God promised we would receive His covenant-based overflowing grace (unmerited favor) and the free gift of righteousness [putting us into right standing with Himself].

    - When we get His overflowing grace, we receive and enjoy grace-based acceptable benefits and the ability to benefit from being deemed acceptable.

    - It also means we have a source of favor, and that which affords joy, pleasure, delight, sweetness, loveliness; all of which is unmerited.

Reign as kings in life through the one Man Jesus Christ (the Messiah, the Anointed One)...

- Through accepting Jesus as our Messiah, our Covenant King, death no longer reigns over us. The tables are turned and now we do the reigning in life as one of the kings that the King of kings is King of. It does not mean we all sit on thrones. It means that we have His authority to make the decrees and proclamations that become law in the realm of each life. It is now the law of life and light in Christ, not the law of sin and death that is reigning. We have been translated into the Kingdom where we have His permission to use His authority to dispel the darkness, enabling His Kingdom to come and His will to be done on earth as it is in Heaven.

Well then, as one man's trespass [one man's false step and falling away led] to condemnation for all men...

- This verse is underscoring that Adam's one unrighteous act of disobedience against the terms of their covenant is the original sin that leads to all others. It is what led to all of his covenant heirs, all mankind, to inherit sin and death. Adam was found guilty as charged and received the specific punishment that he was warned would be the result of his transgression.

So one Man's act of righteousness [leads] to acquittal and right standing with God and life for all men.

- The one Man is Jesus who is also referred to in scripture as the Second Adam. The action taken by the Second Adam is the only way to overturn the prior verdict against the First Adam, bringing acquittal to all of His heirs, all who accept Jesus as their Covenant Maker. His righteous act of offering up His life as the sacrificial lamb to ratify the New and Better Blood Covenant does away with the penalties associated with the original sin and all sin that followed.

- Covenant grace has provided what no attempt to just refrain from sinning as much as possible could ever provide. You now have right standing with God.

These verses are the Seeds that bear the fruit of the Truth that will set you free. You will not automatically and immediately be made perfect in the flesh, but His covenant promise is that you are no longer considered a sinner regardless of what you do or do not do to improve yourself. You will now be treated by Father God exactly as if you are no longer a sinner because you have accepted His blood covenant grace.

✠

This is the mindset that God was just dying to give you:
You are not just a sinner saved by grace.
You were just a sinner, but now you have a new identity.
You are a new creation, a grace-gifted righteous child of God.

✠

A man who was poor and then inherits a great deal of wealth is no longer a poor man. He was poor, but now he is wealthy. You were a sinner, but now you are an inheritor of righteousness.

Abraham was a sinful idolater from a heathen nation. He obtained righteousness, just like us, as a covenant gift from God. On the basis of the blood covenant, God accounted him as righteous. Abraham then lied in ways that could have been punished by death *after* being accounted righteous. He committed sins that not only offended God, but also earthly kings. God had to step in and warn the Kings that Abraham had told a half-lie and not to take his wife or his life. Yet, sins racked up after making a covenant with God did not disqualify him from being accounted righteous because his righteousness was a covenant gift, not a result of human perfection.

It is only understanding the mystery of grace-based blood covenants that can free us from feeling like unworthy sinners who are only pretending to have a new nature. We may still feel unworthy because we know we did not earn or achieve perfection in our flesh. But our unmerited worthiness is not based on how we feel about it.

Our position in Christ is based upon what God said and Jesus did to change our identity from that of being in a broken covenant by natural birth with Adam, to being reborn into the New Covenant with Jesus. The result is to inherit what is ours by blood-covenant grace. We have a new nature, an amazing inheritance, by virtue of the role of grace in our relationship with God.

✠

If the grace that is the basis for our new life in Christ as blood-bought covenant children of God is not all that its definition says it is, then the original Greek text used the wrong word more than 136 times.

✠

The revelation of covenant grace increases exponentially your potential for experiencing the abundant life Jesus promised. You are now free to accept the offer of right standing with God based upon accepting His grace-based blood covenant.

Lord, I believe; help my unbelief.[40]

I know one might think what we have seen here is too good to be true. We must not doubt the Bible while we are learning to quell our unrenewed mind's kibitzing. The secret is to renew your mind with the washing of the water of the Word. Specifically, here are three powerful and fun ways to renew and keep renewing your mind. Wash, rinse, and repeat.

In Christ

The term "In Christ" is a covenant term. It is found all through the New Testament. It literally means to be accepted into, adopted into the family of God, by blood covenant. Almighty God is still Almighty God, but now He also happens to be your Abba Father, your Dad. It is by being in blood covenant with Jesus that you are, "in Christ." Take any

---

[40] (Mark 9:24)

"in Christ" scripture that comes your way and mentally amplify it with the phrase "**covenant with.**" This will reinforce your new relationship as shown by example here: "For as in Adam all die, even so in (**covenant with**) Christ shall all be made alive" (1 Corinthians 15:22 KJV).

Covenant Lord

The fact that the term Lord is a covenant term, meaning the covenant head or covenant lord, is lost on most of us. This will really help. Just insert in your mind, every time you see the word Lord used in scripture referring to Jesus or God, add the word "**Covenant.**" For example: "The grace of our (**Covenant**) Lord Jesus Christ be with you" (1 Corinthians 16:23 KJV).

Grace Scripture Immersion

Open a Bible Concordance or use an online version such as Bible. com. Limit the search criteria to the New Testament and do a search for the term "grace." Not every hit will be helpful, but more than a hundred will be. Rather than read the whole chapter, which is certainly good for normal study, just hop from verse to verse reinforcing the concept of grace being the bedrock of our relationship with Jesus. I recommend doing this with the Amplified Classic Version because it often adds nuances of the meaning of the word grace in the context of the verse.

Here, in no particular order, are just a few examples:

> For it is by free **grace** (God's unmerited favor) that you are saved (delivered from judgment and made partakers of Christ's salvation) through [your] faith. And this [salvation] is not of yourselves [of your own doing, it came not through your own striving], but it is the gift of God. (Ephesians 2:8 AMPC)

*But He said to me, My **grace** (My favor and loving-kindness and mercy) is enough for you [sufficient against any danger and enables you to bear the trouble manfully]. (2 Corinthians 12:9 AMPC)*

*And the Word (Christ) became flesh (human, incarnate) and tabernacled (fixed His tent of flesh, lived awhile) among us; and we [actually] saw His glory (His honor, His majesty), such glory as an only begotten son receives from his father, full of **grace** (favor, loving-kindness) and truth. [Isa. 40:5.] (John 1:14 AMPC)*

*For sin shall not [any longer] exert dominion over you, since now you are not under Law [as slaves], but under **grace** [as subjects of God's favor and mercy]. (Romans 6:14 AMPC)*

*But by the **grace** (the unmerited favor and blessing) of God I am what I am, and His **grace** toward me was not [found to be] for nothing (fruitless and without effect). In fact, I worked harder than all of them [the apostles], though it was not really I, but the **grace** (the unmerited favor and blessing) of God which was with me. (1 Corinthians 15:10 AMPC)*

*For the **grace** of God (His unmerited favor and blessing) has come forward (appeared) for the deliverance from sin and the eternal salvation for all mankind. (Titus 2:11 AMPC)*

*[All] are justified and made upright and in right standing with God, freely and gratuitously by His **grace***

(His unmerited favor and mercy), through the redemption which is [provided] in Christ Jesus. (Romans 3:24 AMPC)

*Let us then fearlessly and confidently and boldly draw near to the throne of **grace** (the throne of God's unmerited favor to us sinners), that we may receive mercy [for our failures] and find **grace** to help in good time for every need [appropriate help and well-timed help, coming just when we need it].* (Hebrews 4:16 AMPC)

Key Points: Review and Reflect

What is the difference between "saving grace" and "blood-covenant grace?"

What can limit the extent to which we can experience the blessings proclaimed to be ours in Matthew 5:8?

Both who we now are and who we once were, are in the Bible. In what way might it benefit us to focus entirely on who and what the Bible says we are now that we have a blood-covenant relationship with God, instead of who and what it says we once were?

Have your expectations of a blessed life perhaps been hampered by a limited revelation of His grace?

I shared three ways I use to help renew my mind to our new grace-based Covenant Mindset. Let me challenge you to do a little experiment. Try one of them for a few weeks, then journal your results.

Your feedback is always welcome at
DanielJDonaldson.com.

-9-

Enjoying Covenant Faith

✠

What are the three covenant secrets to having a
great level of faith and an extremely effective prayer life?

The Bible reveals the One who created us and our world in all of its wonder and infinite complexity. Think of how much being chock full of faith in Him can improve the quality of this life and the life to come. It is learning how to become absolutely full of faith in God that deserves our utmost attention.

✠

There is a strong correlation between the level of faith
you have in Father God, Jesus, and the Holy Spirit,
and the amount of enjoyment that comes from
having a relationship with Them in your life.

✠

You can have a relationship with God that is more comfortable, honest, non-judgmental, intimate, friendly, highly enjoyable, and unpretentious than you could possibly have with any human companion.

✠

**Jesus said, "I have come that your joy and gladness
may be of full measure and complete and overflowing."**[41]

✠

The level of joy we experience in our relationship with the Lord, that He clearly wants us to have, will be in direct relationship to the level of faith we have in Him. When Jesus tells you that He wants your joy to be full, He means that He wants the level, like the amount of gas in your tank, to be full. The same concept of incremental levels of fullness can be a measuring stick for the level of your faith. This is why I enjoy unveiling the *secret to enjoying covenant faith—to the full.*

When it comes to God, you can have **no faith level.** This is like your gas tank being bone-dry empty. The heathen do not know Him because they covenant to serve gods they have made of earth's elements of fire, wood, water, and stone. Those vehicles will get you nowhere you would want to go.

You can have **a little faith,** which would be like being down to less than a quarter of a tank. This is similar to the disciples who did know Him, but did not really understand Him during His earthly ministry. To keep the analogy going, their faith was full enough to get them in the boat and off the shore, but not full enough to get them to the other side of the lake. They ran out when they needed it the most.

You can also have **blind faith.** The gauge is broken—there is some faith in the tank because your motor is still running. However, there is no way to tell if there is enough in the tank or not—which could leave you stranded. Many Christians today faithfully believe in a prescribed set of religious teachings from childhood and are just coasting along. However, when confronted with a steep hill or a rough road, their blind faith is not enough to endure and go the distance. The Bible promises you that you do not have to be driving blind. You can have a **great or a high level of faith.**

---

[41] John 15:11 (AMPC)

✠

**A great level of faith is like having a full tank
of gas or a fully charged battery in your Tesla.**

✠

A full faith level powers you through any obstacle, gets you safely to your destination, and there is joy in the journey. Abraham had this level of faith by virtue of his understanding of the nature and trustworthiness of Father God through His grace, love, and faith-based covenant.

You can have the same topped-off full, high-octane faith Paul obtained. Jesus took Paul aside for three years and taught him the revelation of our New and Better Covenant in Christ,[42] so that he in turn could share it with us. I hope I do not overuse this analogy, but we should see the New Testament as our faith level filling station and go there often for a refill.

We see stories of Bible characters who had great levels of faith and others, not so much. We would all like to have mountain-moving levels of faith, but how? We might think in natural human terms that we would just have to deny ourselves, and fight fiercely, as if we were setting a spiritual goal equivalent to losing a hundred pounds. On the contrary, I am telling you that you cannot and should not try to work hard enough to muster up faith. Why not? Because what you can do by your own strength will **not** increase your ability to trust in Father God instead of yourself.

Contrary to some popular beliefs, fasting, vows of abstinence or poverty, human will power, and fierce effort are **not** the way to fill your faith tank. This is one of the more important secrets to enjoying covenant-based faith. We make a mistake when we equate building faith like we would build up muscles by the serious sweat of our brows. By the muscle measure mindset, faith giants would look like Goliath. However, we know that Goliath was trusting in his massive armor, weapons, and flesh. David, the true faith giant, was an unarmored young lad trusting in his covenant as the source of his great level of faith.

---

[42] Galatians 1:17

A covenant child with a full faith level is like Jesus when confronted by a person displaying dangerous levels of demonic antics. You calmly, but with authority, say what the Word says concerning the situation. There is no need for fanfares, emotional appeals, or bravado.

A covenant-faith propelled journey is like filling your tank with high octane gas, turning the ignition key, and driving the enjoyable road trip from Paris, across southern France, and then back to Paris. The human works-based alternative is to train for months, building up the muscles in your legs, summoning iron will, and mental toughness, so you can peddle your bicycle across the same route. If you work hard enough and catch a few breaks, you could win the Tour de France, to the praise of men. You could also break a leg, succumb to the lure of performance-enhancing drugs, and end up not even finishing the race. The covenant faith-based journey leaves no room for boasting. The vehicle of faith did all the work and you just went along for the ride.

✠

**Potent and effective levels of faith
are based on a covenant relationship.**

✠

Christians without covenant understanding may have blind faith in the phrases they were taught in Sunday School. "The blood of Jesus saves you." When confronted with, "Why do you believe that?" The answer might be, "Because that is what we were taught." The problem is we live in a world averse to faith in Jesus and blind faith might not stand up to testing. The same brat who told you your parents lied to you about Santa Claus, now says, "Didn't they also tell you to have blind faith in the popes being infallible, indulgences literally buying a ticket out of purgatory, and wine literally turning into physical blood?" When faith in those religious constructs proves foolish, blind faith can lead to throwing out the Christ Child with the baptismal bathwater.

✠

**The enemy knows how important faith is.
That is why he tries so hard to make it seem like
great levels of faith require both very hard work and a giant
blind leap, rather than being a very light burden and one small step.**

✠

The forces of the darkened world use contrary circumstances, half-truths, outright lies, and misinformation to undermine mankind's ability to have great levels of faith. After all, has that not always been the enemy's primary and effective tactic throughout human history?

> *And the serpent said to the woman, ye shall not surely die.
> For God doth know that in the day ye eat thereof, then
> your eyes shall be opened, and you shall be as gods...."*
> (Genesis 3:4 KJV)

The enemy assaults us with twisting of words, questioning, injecting fear, uncertainty, and doubt. He offers an alternative reason for God's motivation. Distrust quickly leads to disobedience.

✠

**It is faith in the blood covenant that can give us a way
to confound the enemy, trust the unseen God's
promises, and take Him at His Word.**

✠

We only need to develop great faith in one thing—what it means to be in a loving blood-covenant relationship with Father God and Jesus Christ. Once we get the revelation of how blood covenants work, we can put our full faith, our trust, and our confidence in our Covenant Makers and Their covenant promises. God the Father and Jesus Christ will never break the covenant, which is why it will remain in full effect and force for eternity.

The New and Better Covenant is not dependent on mankind keeping all of His laws perfectly. In terms of this unique covenant agreement, it is only needful for us to believe and have faith in *His* ability to make and keep the covenant. It is only this belief, not our perfection, which delivers to us the perfection we need to be acceptable in His sight. The blood covenant is the reason we can believe and have sufficient faith to receive all of the promises made to those in covenant with Christ.

For faith to be effective, it has to be able to endure. This is another reason I like the measuring stick for faith being like measuring the level of gas in your tank. For those with electric cars, it would be the battery charge level. Relative levels are no faith (tank on empty), a little faith (less than a quarter tank), blind faith (gas level gauge not working), strong faith (more than half a tank), or max out the scale with great faith, a full tank. If you are not going far, a little gas in the tank, or not even being able to tell how much is in there, may still get you by. But remember the discomfort of owning a car that does not always start. Without knowing you have enough faith petrol in your tank for the trip, you are not going to enjoy the ride.

What are the three covenant secrets to having your tank full of faith in God, and an extremely effective prayer life?

We know Abraham had a full and effective level of faith, but how exactly did he get it? God knew Abraham would be on a very long faith journey and needed a full tank of faith at the outset and a way to continue to refill it, to go the distance. God used three elements of covenant-making to top off Abraham's faith tank. It seems to have worked nicely, so let's also "Fill her up" by using these same three covenant secrets. We will then have that great level of faith in our tank that can take us anywhere we want to go. We will see how this can help us offer up more effective prayers. Bolstered by full faith and covenant standing with God, we will have an extremely effective prayer life.

✠

The secret behind the secrets, words matter.

✠

Death and life are in the power of the tongue, and they
who indulge in it shall eat the fruit of it [for death or life].
(Proverbs 18:21 AMPC)

There is another powerful mystery to making a covenant that under-
lies all the ways Father God designed for our covenant-making to change
our lives. It lies in the power *behind* the power of the covenant oath. God
made us in His likeness. One of those likenesses is to have vested in man
the same power to create, rule, and reign over his realm using the power
and authority of a speaking spirit to proclaim things. If there was no power
or force in our words, then a covenant would mean nothing because what
you say would not matter. However, the crux of any covenant is based upon
what you say when you proclaim your covenant oaths, and it does matter.
Covenant makers add the element of life and death by adding blood to the
ceremony. If you do not act in a way that corresponds to your stated covenant vows, death and calamity are waiting in the wings.

Often, the verse above is used to pull us up short as a warning, but that
need not be. It just says you get to choose life or death by choosing what
you say. This is how faith works its miracle power. What you hear you tend
to believe. What you believe you tend to say. What you say you will have
(like it or not).

We often say what we do not mean and do not mean what we say,
confusing our spirit and eroding confidence in the power of our words.
Devout Christians believe that you can change your eternal destiny by
merely confessing with your mouth and believing in your heart that Jesus
is the Messiah, Lord. Yet, many discount the value and importance of all
the other words they say. "That preacher was so anointed; his message just
thrilled me to death." "I know, the next meeting is going to be awesome. I
was tickled to death to get tickets." "Those kids are doing it again. I swear

137

they are going to be the death of me." "I laughed so hard, I thought I was going to die." "You know, every time our vacation time comes around, I get sick; if it is not one thing, it's another." "My sinuses always act up this time of year."

Notice that happy or sad, good times or bad, we have been fooled into using an expression in our language that incorporates death and calamity into our response to life. It is natural to want to spice up our conversations, but this is no joke. What we say even in jest is being used to seriously shape our world.

Fortunately, God used the truth behind the power of covenant words for good, to increase Abraham's faith level. Specifically, let's see three ways God uses words to work life and faith into Abraham's and our covenant-conscious spirits.

Secret #1: The Blood Covenant

Abraham was already beginning to trust God before there was a covenant between them. Abraham (prior to the covenant named Abram), would hear and then act on what God told him in visions and it worked out well. However, the final promise of a child to inherit needed to be backed up by more than a voice in his head. The hard facts were his wife's inability to conceive and his inability to conceive how in her old age she ever could. What God promised would be years away in coming. God provided the assurance Abraham needed by cutting a blood covenant with him. Knowing that to break a blood covenant is to court death, the impracticality of the promise withered away. Abraham could now believe, trust, and have faith in God delivering what He promised with His spoken covenant oath.

This is the underlying message of the Old Testament, the New Testament, and this book. The number one covenant secret to having great faith is to know what it means to be in a blood covenant relationship with God. The covenant relationship we have with Father God and our Covenant Head Jesus is new and better than all that went before. Neither the Father nor the Son will ever break their covenant words, making it eternal. All we have to do is accept entrance into the covenant relationship through accepting its blood sacrifice, the blood of Jesus. When we partake of communion, we are reenacting and bringing to remembrance the covenant-meal ceremony. We are now in covenant with Christ.

You can have great levels of faith in God because blood covenant tells you who He is, what He has done, what compelled Him to offer you the covenant (love), and what you can expect Him to do going forward (keep His promises).

✠

**Father God will adopt you and you will inherit
all the promises you have faith to receive.**

✠

This is the key. You will not enjoy what you do not realize you have a covenant right to inherit. You cannot demonstrate by your holiness or any other virtue that you are thus more worthy of covenant promises. You only need to have great faith in His having accepted you into His covenant and that He has given the promises to you by grace.

> *For this is My blood of the new covenant, which [ratifies the agreement and] is being poured out for many for the forgiveness of sins.* (Matthew 26:28 AMPC)

Secret #2: The Name Changer

The covenant ceremony absolutely took the relationship between God and Abraham to a whole new level. Yet, there were many years before the promise would be fulfilled. What could God do to remind Abraham of His promises every day and make his faith grow stronger over time rather than weaker? The second secret to having great faith is to see what a game-changer it is to have your name changed. This is crystal clear in weddings which are blood-covenant ceremonies. Names are changed and added together, so that all now know these two have become as one.

God changed Abram's name to Abraham, changing its meaning from *Exalted Father* to *Father of Nations*. His human father gave him a good name that he hoped would help him grow into being revered. God has now given him this new name so that he could grow into it. This is part of the process of instilling and bolstering Abraham's faith in the covenant promise God made to him. It's like having a fuel truck following you, adding more fuel while you are still driving.

Do you now see the benefit of having the new names the Bible uses to describe His covenanted ones? The new name is not aside from the covenant, it is because of the covenant. Our new names are a blueprint for believing and having faith to enjoy who we now are, in covenant with Christ.

✠

**We will not be saints someday; we are now saints.
We are now called New Creatures. We are now His Body,
Kings and Priests of His Kingdom, Children of God,
the Apple of His Eye, the Accepted in the Beloved,
the Redeemed, Healed, and Delivered.**

✠

Use your names like Abraham did. While still childless, Abraham was *already* being called *Father of Nations*. While still imperfect, you are already called the Righteous. While still showing symptoms of sickness, you are the Healed. Jesus also says let the weak say, I am strong; let the poor say, I am rich. By the very act of calling yourself what He has called you, you are becoming like who He says you already are.

Secret #3: WYSIWYG

WYSIWYG, (pronounced wizzy wig), means What You See is What You Get. It means what you see on your PC screen is what you will get when you print the image on paper. It is also a good acronym to describe how faith is refueled with what we envision.

The natural eye and the mind's eye are powerful forces that can enrich or not enrich our lives, depending on what we choose to spend our time seeing. It works just like words do, for better or for worse. What you see and keep on seeing is what you are going to get and keep on getting. If you do not like what you see around you in the natural, in your mind's eye, see a better version of your life as you would have it. What you see with the eyes of faith will one day manifest to your natural eyes.

The process is even more effective if you are directed to use something you can see with your natural eyes to focus on what God wants you to see with your mind's eye. God knew there would be a long time between the promise of a son and Abraham seeing his newborn with his natural eyes. In the interim, God gave him something to envision, to see before seeing.

> *And He brought him outside [his tent into the starlight] and said, Look now toward the heavens and count the stars—if you are able to number them. Then He said to him, So shall your descendants be.* (Genesis 15:5 AMPC)

God also told Abraham to look at the grains of sand, just in case it was an overcast night, and count them. What you see is what you get. When we look at the Hebrew children being Abraham's heirs and all the gentiles who are being grafted into the same family tree, we can clearly see the vision coming to pass.

What can we use as a pattern for envisioning what Father God has promised us? What can we see with our natural eyes that will help us visualize with our mind's eye the great promises that are our covenant inheritance?

We can fix our eyes on the written promises and the many benefits of our covenant relationship in the Bible. As an example, I recommend seeing and hearing yourself say the first six verses of Psalm 103. Speak these verses daily over yourself. Rehearsing what you are seeing audibly harnesses the power of what you are seeing, saying, and hearing. When you see what it says, you will begin to believe what you see. When you say what it says about you, you will begin to believe what you hear and say. We tend to believe some of what others say and most of what we say. When we hear us saying it, we really put the power of our words to work filling the faith tank.

> *BLESS (AFFECTIONATELY, gratefully praise) the Lord,*
> *O my soul; and all that is [deepest] within me, bless His*
> *holy name!*
>
> *Bless (affectionately, gratefully praise) the Lord, O my soul,*
> *and forget not [one of] all His benefits—*
>
> *Who forgives [every one of] all your iniquities,*
>
> *Who heals [each one of] all your diseases,*
>
> *Who redeems your life from the pit and corruption,*
>
> *Who beautifies, dignifies, and crowns you with loving-kind-*
> *ness and tender mercy,*
>
> *Who satisfies your mouth [your necessity and desire at your*
> *personal age and situation] with good so that your youth,*
> *renewed, is like the eagle's [strong, overcoming, soaring]!*
>
> *The Lord executes righteousness and justice [not for me only,*
> *but] for all who are oppressed. (Psalm 103:1-6 AMPC)*

Prayers that Avail Much

✠

**The more you see yourself the way Jesus sees you,
the more the world will see Him in you and through you.**

✠

I hope I have given insight into who we are in covenant with Christ and increased your faith in our blood covenant with Him. This is not a selfish proposition. We are told to go out and proclaim the Gospel of the Blood Covenant to all people. We cannot tell others just how good it is unless we understand and take hold of just how good it is for ourselves. Before we take off, our flight attendants always tell us in the case of an emergency we are to put the mask on ourselves first, so that we will remain conscious and be able to help others. Wise council.

One of the most effective ways to deliver results for ourselves and others is in our prayer life. Developing great and effective faith in the covenant and the Covenant Maker will transform our prayer life.

We saw previously how there is a benefit to having saving grace and a far greater benefit to having an understanding of what it means to have covenant grace. The same thing applies here. There is a certain benefit to knowing you are saved by the blood of Jesus. I call this "saving faith." There is exponentially more potential for enjoying your relationship with Father God, Jesus, and the Holy Spirit when you know that it is a covenant-based relationship and you develop faith in having a blood covenant with God. I call this "covenant faith."

Here is just a quick glimpse at how covenant faith transforms your spiritual life and prayers. If you have "saving faith," you know you are saved, but since you still sin, you may think it inappropriate to call yourself entirely righteous. You may not be comfortable asserting that you are just as righteous as Jesus, as righteous as if you never sinned. We can tell how you feel about this by your prayers. The following quote was taken verbatim from the overhead screen at a church. It was the corporate prayer following a sermon on how to be more committed to witnessing for Jesus. The pastor asked the congregation to rise and all say this with her:

> *"Heavenly Father, we confess that we fall prey to apathy. We often live our lives on our own terms acting as though You do not matter. Rather than being excited and on fire in our service to You, we have become lukewarm Christians."*

Even if some of it is true for some standing there, falling prey to apathy is certainly not true of all of them. It was at a Sunday Church Service, not a spring break motorcycle rally. Furthermore, you may think you are being humble, but you are saying what the old man is like, not describing the new creation. Why isn't everyone in that church out saving souls? Perhaps, they spent too much time in church and began to believe what they were saying. In contrast, covenant faith speaks this way.

> *Heavenly Father, thank You for the revelation of Your mercy, grace, and blessings that make us zealous to live our lives for You. We are excited and on fire for You. We are empowered by You to be the overcoming and victorious Christians You have made us to be by Your covenant love and for Your glory.*

Use the promises of Father God, your new names, and your new vision of who you are in Christ to put high octane faith in your tank and power in your prayers.

Key Points: Review and Reflect

What is the difference between "saving faith" and "blood covenant faith?"

What can increase our faith in the promises proclaimed to be ours in Matthew 5:8?

Father God gave us names that we can speak over ourselves to remind us who we are instead of who we were. Which names help you the most in obtaining your new identity in covenant with Christ and why?

Have your expectations of a blessed life perhaps been hampered by a limited revelation of covenant faith?

What are the three covenant secrets God provides to help us become people of great faith?

Continue to record in your journal how the impact of what you are learning is affecting your life.

Your feedback is always welcome at
DanielJDonaldson.com.

-10-

Enjoying Covenant Favor

✠

How can you have the happiness produced by experiencing God's favor?

Blessed *(happy, enviably fortunate, and spiritually prosperous—**possessing the happiness produced by the experience of God's favor** and especially **conditioned by the revelation of His grace**, regardless of their outward conditions) are the pure in heart, for they shall see God!* (Matthew 5:8 AMPC emphasis added)

An important part of the blessings that accompany our covenant relationship is the experience of God's favor. However, take note, there is a direct correlation between our happily experiencing God's favor and the prerequisite revelation of His grace. As we explore how to enjoy covenant grace, faith, and favor, it is not an accident that grace comes first. Covenant favor no longer needs to be curried apart from grace; it is a byproduct of it.

For You, O LORD, will bless the righteous;
*With **favor** You will surround him as with a shield.*

(Psalm 5:12 emphasis added)

The laws of obtaining favor have not changed. In order to get Part B, having favor surround you, you must qualify by being Part A, the righteous. What has changed is that the grace-based blood covenant has made you righteous apart from anything you could do to earn it. If you do not understand this vital point concerning God's favor being like showers of blessings, it might seem unpredictable like rain falling here or there, or unobtainable because you are not righteous enough. Some might not put it into words, but they are uncomfortable with the concept of actually pursuing the favor of God. For some, just asking God to give you favor smacks of greed and inappropriate pursuit of material blessings. These are examples of what I call "myth-understandings." They have been around so long that myth cloaks their origin. They are commonly held or popular beliefs based upon half-truths, and shared personal experiences. Part of revealing mysteries is to dispel myths with the truth.

"A myth is true only some of the time, for some people, and in some situations. An irrefutable truth is rooted in God's Word which is true for all people, all the time, and in all situations." – Dr. Larry Keefauver

To help unveil the irrefutable truth that grace is what now qualifies us to enjoy favor, we need to know that the English word "favor" in the Bible is based on the Greek word *charis*. Yes, this is the same word translated as *grace* in some instances and as *favor in other passages*. The words are not interchangeable, but they have much in common. When Father God is showing us favor, He does so by grace. When Jesus is doing something for us, He is gracing us with His favor. When God initiates the favor, it is provided to us by Father God without our having earned it. We call this unmerited favor and unmerited grace.

As was true of "grace," *favor* also means to receive acceptable benefits, the ability to benefit from being deemed acceptable. It also means to be given that which affords joy, pleasure, delight, sweetness, loveliness; all of which are unmerited gifts. The definition also includes what you can expect from someone showing *hessed*, a covenant term for receiving God's loving-kindness and tender mercy.

You may not have thought about it in these terms before. The greatest "favor" Jesus ever did for us was to become our blood-covenant sacrifice, making it possible for us to accept His blood covenant. His actions fit the definition of a covenant favor. Jesus gladly did it for the express purpose of benefiting us. He died for us of His own free will and we did not deserve it.

The Favor of Kings

God uses kings making rulings in the Bible to teach us one aspect of how covenant favor works. Most of us have heard how Esther was understandably fearful of the prospect of going, unsolicited, to have an audience with King Ahasuerus. In biblical times and far into later centuries, a King presiding over his court would sit on his throne with a scepter in hand. The scepter represented his authority and right to rule. If a person approached him unbidden, for any reason, one of two things would happen. He would either extend the scepter toward that person, thereby showing favor and grace, or he does not extend it and the person's life is forfeit.

We know the king extended his scepter and favor to Esther, but there is more. There is a second benefit that is just as important, if not more so. Once the king rules in your favor, you never look back to your former life or fear him changing his mind. The decree that shows you favor is not only advantageous, it is just as permanent as the word of the King.

✠

Apart from the grace-based covenant, the one seeking favor had to show just cause for receiving it.

✠

149

There are times when God chooses to give favor where it is not due because He is a loving and omnipotent God. But the norm for humans seeking favor is to do something to justify asking for it. Esther did not just waltz in and ask the king for the favor she sought, she worked very hard for many months to compel him to love her. The captive slave Joseph worked tirelessly for many years to show himself approved as a servant, as well as in prison, and even shaved and bathed before appearing to curry the favor of the Pharaoh. Each story indicates that they received favor that rewrote their life ever after. The foreign-born girl became Queen. The prisoner Joseph became ruler.

However, grace changes everything. The only thing we have to do to put ourselves in a position to enjoy the favor of God is to accept His grace-based covenant.

✠

The King of kings has extended His cross-shaped scepter toward us.

✠

The cross is the scepter that is extended to us, when by grace, we accept what it did for us. The favor shown to us takes away our beggar's cloak and gives us His robes of righteousness. We are even granted the rarest of favor any king ever granted. We are invited to have a seat beside King Jesus and help Him rule and reign. We never need to come back begging to His court again. Scripture says, come boldly to the throne of *charis*, grace.[43]

The decree that grants you favor is not only advantageous, it is just as permanent as the word of the King. Now that you know that the favor of God is part of your heritage, thank Him for His favor already received and look forward to enjoying more favor than ever before. Just for fun, see yourself getting ready to go to the Lord with

---

[43] Hebrews 4:16

a difficult prayer request. You have studied scripture verses to back up the promises they are based on and you have meditated on receiving favor. Now, having come to the throne of grace, you begin to speak and make your case to the Lord. After a while, Jesus raises His hand and you hold your breath. Jesus then says, "Favored child, relax, you had Me at *Lord*."

Doing Covenant Favors

Father God, the architect of covenant-making, orchestrated how kings rule by laying down the inflexible and unyielding covenant law. Yet, as we have seen, the Lord also made provision for kings to choose to extend unmerited favor and grace when appropriate. There is another aspect to favor and doing favors, which is also bedrock fundamental to our salvation. We saw how Jesus agreed with Father God to do a favor for us, ushering in the way of salvation. Now, consider this. The Father God's plan to offer us salvation was made possible by Him first asking a man to do a favor for Him!

In the Abrahamic Covenant, we have the forerunner of our own grace-based covenant. Father God made promises to Abraham and He delivered on them. Then, God surprised everyone by asking Abraham to do something unthinkable. It was not a required part of the covenant. It was not required to receive the things already promised and being given to Abraham. God asked Abraham to do something for Him as a seriously big favor. Abraham could decide to do or not to do what was asked of him. God did not have to explain why He asked him to do such a hard thing. These are all tenets of asking for a favor from a covenant partner.

Abraham was not comfortable with God's plan to destroy all of Sodom and started bartering, tried to get God to change His mind, and lower the bar. But here, what is asked flies in the face of the promise of heirs by the one he is asked to kill. Why no push back? Abraham knew this was a specific favor being asked of him by his covenant partner, and if it was not important to God for him to do this favor, He would not have asked. There is another cardinal rule to covenant favors which enabled Abraham to gladly do the unthinkable.

✠

When you ask a covenant favor, you are obligating yourself to do likewise, returning a like favor in exchange, in due time, is not optional.

✠

By making the request, Abraham knew God was obligating Himself to do a comparable favor in return. In fact, the Book of Hebrews tells us how Abraham thought God was going to return the favor.[44] Abraham expected the return favor to be God raising Isaac from the dead. God's plan was far more important and on a whole different scale. By obligating Himself to do a similar, but greater favor, God secretly effected the legal substitution of the death of His own Son for Abraham's and all mankind.

I reprised that story here to show how Father God provides a way for His children to enjoy doing covenant favors for Him and receiving favors in return from Him. There are many other examples of Old Testament prophets, patriarchs, and Jesus asking people to do a favor. The prophet of God asked the starving woman to make him a meal first with the little food she had left. Result? The woman was provided food for the balance of the famine by the prophet. Jesus asked to use the fisherman's boat to preach to the crowd on the shoreline. Result? A boat teeming with fish when none were caught earlier that day was the return favor Jesus did for the fisherman. Our mission is to finish what Jesus started, so it is only fitting that He continues to ask us to show Him favor and receive favor in return. This is part of the body doing what the head asks us to do for Him of our own free will.

---

[44] Hebrews 11:17-19

✠

**Doing covenant favors is the secret to participating
in the grace-based covenant with our works;
a way which is not inappropriately trying
to add works to the salvation equation.**

✠

Have you wondered how doing good works fit into the grace covenant? We know we are saved by grace, but deep down we also know there are good things we feel we should be doing like they did in the Bible. But what if the good we do is out of a sense of indebtedness or law? If we still owe a debt, what we do is not a free gift at all, it is paying back a debt we owe. The legal obligation to unsuccessfully serve the law of sin and death was replaced with a way to successfully serve the law of love, grace, and favor.

Grace does not require us to keep ceremonial or dietary laws or add works to attain salvation or holiness. What it does do is free us up to do all that we do as a way to show our favor and love for Father God, Jesus, and the Holy Spirit. If we make a mistake, grace covers us. If we succeed in being a blessing to someone for Him, God gets the glory. The new covenant has us doing good as guided by our heart to favor Him, instead of check-marking a legal requirement on our to-do list.

God asks us to do favors out of love for Him, of our own free will, at the pace of our own physical capabilities, spiritual growth, and maturity. As we do them, we will increase our physical capabilities, spiritual growth, and maturity. Grace will help us to make the free-will choice to favor Jesus over the other people, places, and things in our lives.

Scripture asks you to show love to others, forgive, pray, and give generously. These are what He asks all of us to do who love Him. Jesus also might ask you to stretch yourself. He could ask you to do something that is a bit more challenging, as a special favor, just for Him. If you understand how covenant favors work, this is when it really gets to be fun. He might ask you to give up something totally lawful for you to have, that you really like, for a period of time. Jesus also might ask you to do something hard, something that takes up a lot of your personal time. It might be a job in the church or community that no one else wants or likes to do. This is no substitute for grace. Grace makes your giving a response to love, not a stepping stone to acceptance.

Grace also bestows favors even if you do not do anything to garner them, other than to simply expect them.

On the top of my daily to-do list on my cell phone is this phrase: "Thank you, Lord, for exceeding my expectations today." I do not do anything more than just be aware, anticipate, and look for the unmerited favor He just plain blesses me with, and He does. What a joy to turn around the phrase, "Well, I did not see that coming." Instead of unexpected problems, I look for unexpected favors.

Let me share one example, a personal life-changing event from my own experience. I had worked hard in many other churches, helping them to grow in many ways. When I moved to New Jersey, I thought I could become less involved in a small local church's business and development. I also thought my home mortgage would be next to nothing, selling a very expensive home in California for twice what I owed on it. Long story short, I made the move in 2006 at the very height of the housing crash. My California home lingered on the market, finally selling for about half the amount expected. This created a perfect storm of realty disaster. I had already committed to purchasing and moving into a New Jersey home costing twice what I expected to end up owing, because the bottom fell out of the market before I could sell my California home. Over the course of the twelve years of housing market recovery, the New Jersey home was still steep upside down in debt.

Meanwhile, I was busy traveling the world for my business and taking care of my Imaging System dealers in all fifty states. Yet, I was loudly and clearly being asked by the Lord to double down on my commitment to teach adult Bible classes when at home. I was also asked to volunteer without pay to work just as hard as ever behind the scenes in the local church. My focus, as in other churches, was the financial side of things, and on finding the growing church new land and buildings at least double the original size. The building fund totaled about a tenth of what was needed. It took a lot of donated time and money across all twelve years. Of course, others worked as hard or harder and sacrificed as well.

Before I left New Jersey, a miracle happened. God revealed how we could supernaturally sell our church home in a timely manner, for more than we owed, at the top of the market, and buy the perfect new church home at a fraction of its value, in a timely manner, for an amount we could well afford.

I was completely overjoyed at this, while completely under-joyed by the imminent, seemly impossible, property buying and selling situation I was personally facing. I could no longer afford to live in New Jersey after my planned retirement in 2018. I could not sell my home for more than the remaining mortgage and I would have no money to put down to purchase a new home in South Carolina.

I was driving down Cross Keys Road in front of our church's old property, and the Voice of the Lord spoke to my heart. "Thank you, Daniel, for doing Me the favor of helping to supernaturally negotiate for the buying and selling of My church homes. Because you put Me and My houses first and did this favor for Me, I am going to return the favor. I will see to it that although it looks like you will have to be foreclosed on and walk away still owning debt even bankruptcy cannot remove, it will not happen. I will help you sell your home in a timely manner, at the top of the market, at a price you can well afford to accept. There will be no bankruptcy and no residual debt. You will be able to qualify for and I will then show you the perfect new home for your family in South Carolina; at a price you can well afford." It was not easy, but God made every impossible situation melt away, and I am typing from the comfort of my new home's office in Lexington, South Carolina.

God may not ask of you what fit my situation, but after many years of living by faith, grace, and the blood covenant, I was glad, eager, and happy to do it. I did not expect to need what I needed. I thought after twelve years, the home would be completely recovered from its upside-down status. God saw my need well in advance and asked me to sow long and often before I needed the crop's mega harvest of favor.

I have only shared one of the epic miracles that the favor of God has delivered to me. I encourage you to find ways to do Father God as big a favor as possible. You never know when you are going to need Him to return the favor, but I have it on good authority that He will do so.

Key Points: Review and Reflect

What are the implications of the same Greek word being translated sometimes as grace and other times as favor?

What are the two ways that the oath of a covenant king benefits the one who curries the king's favor?

If works will not add to your salvation by grace, why do them?

Why does Father God ask you to do things that are very difficult for you to do, as a favor, but having no bearing on your salvation?

What favor is Jesus asking you to do that is a hard thing for you?

How does it change your perspective on doing the things Father God asks you to do, now knowing His hidden purpose is to obligate Himself to return the favor?

Could you now kick up a notch the way you look at doing and receiving favors with others?

What if someone is asking you to do a favor? Instead of expecting a repayment of favor by the person, what if you do it as if unto the Lord, and then look to the Lord rather than the one in need to return the favor?

Continue to record in your journal how the impact of what you are learning is affecting your life.

Your feedback is always welcome at DanielJDonaldson.com.

-11-

The Threshold Covenant

*Why does Jesus, who can walk
through walls, stand at your door and knock?*

There is a whole body of truth concerning making blood covenants that have not had as much attention in books on this subject as it ought. All of the characteristics and practices we have seen hold true in what we will now explore, but there is more. One word to sum up the deeper truths and value about to be revealed is a word often used to explain why a home of similar size and qualities of another can command a dramatically higher price: location, location, location.

I do not mean in the sense of country or locale because this type of covenant ceremony, like others we have referenced, has been conducted in all parts of the world, by all ancient cultures. Several vestiges of this type of the covenant-making ceremony remain to this day in weddings and other meaningful events around the world.

The location I refer to is a part of the physical doorway, the primary entrance to a home, church, temple, or city. The word associated with this location has continued to be used long after the initial purpose became obsolete.

For a millennium, the homes of most people had earthen surfaces. Wood was far too valuable to lay on the ground and not easily crafted into thin layers. The soft, yet otherwise worthless byproduct of separating grain from plants by treading or threshing is called thresh. Placing thresh in the home was an easy way to improve the flooring, but a way was needed to hold the thresh inside the home. The "threshold" was a physical barrier of stone or wood separating thresh which was to stay inside, from everything else which was to remain outside.

The doorway of the house, church, temple, or city became a sacred location. Court was held at the gates of the city. To get to sit at the city gates was a point of honor and a sign of respect. Likewise, doorways separated what part of the temple area could be entered and by whom. The architecture of early churches was also divided by how far inside different groups of ecclesiastical members could go. Be it the city, temple, church, or home, only those with authority and permission could enter by passing over the thresholds of certain doorways.

Sacrifices to gods took place at the doorways. The sacrifice was always made outside, and the blood of the sacrifice sprinkled on the posts, lintel (timber or stone placed above the doorposts to support the doorway), and dripping down also onto the threshold (timber or stone placed across the entrance below the door). By doing this, the head of the household, who was also the priest of the home, marked it as a place guarded by their god.[45] Many ancient accounts document and reveal the fear and reverence this gave to doorways. Whether it was invaders of a city or thieves seeking to rob a home, they sought to gain entry through some other way. The idea of the door being well fortified was only part of the decision to find an alternate route inside. The world of spiritual forces was not a thing to trifle with. Interlopers feared to cross

---

[45] *The Threshold Covenant*, Dr. H. Clay Trumbull. Original publish date 1896, ISBN #0-89228-075-1. A compliment to earlier book *The Blood Covenant*, the primary historical scholarly reference book on the subject of blood covenants.

the blood-sprinkled doorway known to be protected by the dweller's deity, lest doing so would bring a curse upon them.[46]

The spiritual significance and importance of the threshold to a place of worship is revealed in an amazing passage from 1 Samuel. Israel lost a battle with the Philistines that resulted in their capturing the Ark of the Covenant, the most holy possession of Israel. The Ark held the artifacts representing the Mosaic Covenant and was to be placed in the inner-most chamber of their temple. The Philistines decided to demonstrate the superiority of their god that they gave credit to for their victory, placing the Ark of the Covenant inside their temple's holiest chamber beside the statue of Dagon. They chose poorly.

> *And when they arose early on the morrow morning, behold, Dagon was fallen upon his face to the ground before the ark of the Lord; and the head of Dagon and both the palms of his hands were cut off **upon the threshold**; only the stump of Dagon was left to him. Therefore neither the priests of Dagon nor any that come into Dagon's house, **tread on the threshold** of Dagon in Ashdod unto this day.* (1 Samuel 5:4-5 KJV emphasis added)

When it came time to cut blood covenants, such as for a wedding relationship, they held these sacred ceremonies at the doorway of homes. Another such ceremony took place at the doorway of homes when the king of a realm would visit areas under his authority, to find out who in his realm was a loyal subject. The royal would herald his coming and then approach their homes. If a blood covenant sacrifice was evident by the blood on the doorposts and lintel, he knew they were worthy and accepting of his pledge of covenant protection.

When making a threshold covenant, the makers stood outside the home. The sacrifice was made. Blood was applied to the doorposts, lintel,

---

[46] John 10:1

and threshold. The covenanters made oaths outside, in the presence of witnesses. Once covenanted or betrothed, they stepped **over** the threshold. One never stepped **on** the threshold. You only **pass over** it. Some cultures even dictated which foot went first, usually the right foot. This is where we get the term putting your best foot forward. Often, the husband would lift his bride over the threshold lest any part of her garment touch the blood on the threshold. They then would enter and eat the covenant meal inside.

Before entering, they were separate families or king and would-be subjects. After entering, the two cemented the relationship which said, my home and all that lies within it is yours and all that is yours is mine. When the king passed over the threshold, his power, authority, and protection were now in the home. An attack on the home of the subject was an attack on the king. If someone did not agree to be in covenant with the king, if no sacrifice was offered, the king would send his avenging destroyers to remove the offender and his household from his territory.

I am sure you are beginning to see why the ceremony Moses instructed the Hebrew children to conduct on the night of their deliverance from Egypt was not unfamiliar to them. You do not grow from a few hundred to over a million people without conducting more than a few wedding ceremonies at your doorways. The Egyptians worshipped a plethora of gods and marked their homes with the authority of their gods. These were the gods that the God of Israel proved to be false gods by having his plagues defy their power, and then by His destroyer entering their homes by the doorway to take the life of their firstborn, regardless of the false gods honored there.

*Then Moses called for all the elders of Israel, and said unto them, Draw out and take you a lamb according to your families, and kill the **passover**. And ye shall take a bunch of hyssop, and dip it in the blood that is in the basin, and strike the lintel and the two side posts with the blood that is in the basin; and none of you shall go out at the door of his house*

until the morning. For the LORD will pass through to
smite the Egyptians; and when he seeth the blood upon the
lintel, and on the two side posts, the LORD will pass over
*the **door**, and will not suffer the destroyer to come in unto*
your houses to smite you. And ye shall observe this thing
for an ordinance to thee and to thy sons for ever. (Exodus
12:21-24 KJV emphasis added)

What does it mean to **pass-over** in the context of what we have
just learned? This will be a shocking surprise to some, but if you believe
the point requires further study before accepting it, I refer you to the
addendum included in the earlier referenced book by Dr. Turnbull. In
its supplemental commentary, several Jewish theologians and scholars of
the Talmud echo agreement with his conclusion. Along with this scholarly work and with covenant awareness, I read the scriptures and I believe
it is as clear as day.

What is the "passover" referenced in verse 21? Clearly, it is the
Passover ceremony's sacrifice animal, needing no further explanation for
those already familiar with making this type of blood covenant. The use
of the term was synonymous with performing a "pass over the threshold"
blood-covenant ceremony for hundreds of years prior to that night.
Why is the animal a Passover ceremony sacrifice animal? It is because
this animal sacrifice is part of the blood-covenant ceremony conducted
at the threshold of the home. The family and the one covenanting with
them, taking care not to trample the sacred sacrifice blood, "pass over" the
threshold, enter the home, close the door, and eat the covenant meal inside.

Whether the residents saw Him or not, Moses assures them it will be
exactly like all the other Passover ceremonies; the presence of the covenant
maker will join them inside their home and provide covenant protection.
"When he seeth the blood upon the lintel, and on the two side posts (he
does not see the blood on the threshold, because the closed door obscures
it), the LORD will pass over the door (***petah***, doorway, entrance, opening,
threshold) and **come into your home.**" Closed doors may obscure the

threshold, but have never prevented God from going where He is invited in. "The Lord will not suffer the destroyer to come in unto your houses to smite you (the angel of death will pass over the thresholds and enter the homes not marked by the blood of the Passover sacrifice, but will not enter yours)."

Father God is covenanting to be with His people, like a groom crossing the threshold with his bride, to dwell with her there. Now, scores of scriptures referencing His covenant children as His bride make total sense. When they go after other gods, this is depicted as a wife playing the harlot, betraying her husband. He loves her as a husband is instructed to love his wife. I am told the Song of Solomon is recited at Passover Meal celebrations bringing up all the imagery of a king extolling the virtues of the queen he is courting. The Lord will pass over the threshold to enter in and enjoy unbroken fellowship with His bride.

> *And ye shall observe this thing for an ordinance to thee and to thy sons for ever.* (Exodus 12:24 KJV)

Father God knew that it would be a long time before the kind of fellowship and intimacy He ultimately planned to have with the Seed of Abraham would be possible. He ordained they bring this night's threshold blood-covenant ceremony to their remembrance at the outset of each new year. We now call this the Passover Meal. Father God would have them celebrate their partial deliverance and the promise of a Redeemer to come and complete the job in the fullness of time.

In the fullness of time, the Redeemer did indeed come. In the chapter that follows, we see how Jesus used the remembrance of the Passover covenant meal as the backdrop for introducing His New Covenant and how to bring it to our remembrance.

✠

Those who embrace this New Covenant will enjoy the level of grace, faith, favor,

**and fellowship God intended us to have
and have abundantly.**

✠

Jesus will not just point to the entranceway of His kingdom residence; Jesus has become the way of entrance.

> *I am the door: by me if any man enter in, he shall be saved, and shall go in and out, and find pasture. The thief cometh not, but for to steal, and to kill, and to destroy: I am come that they might have life, and that they might have it more abundantly.* (John 10:9-10 KJV)

Key Points: Review and Reflect

How did the Hebrew children know what it meant when Moses told them to kill the passover?

Although often the brunt of jokes now, what is the reason the bride was to be carried over the threshold by the groom?

How does the "pass over the threshold" covenant help us understand God referring to Abraham's spiritual children as His bride? Are we the bride of Christ?

The Israelites placed the blood of the Passover lamb on the post and crossbeam (lintel) of their doors. Where was the blood of Jesus placed?

Why does Jesus, who can walk through walls, stand at your door and knock?

Behold, I stand at the door, and knock: if any man hear my voice, and open the door, I will come in to him, and will sup with him, and he with me. (Revelation 3:20 KJV)

Continue to record in your journal how the impact of what you are learning is affecting your life.

Your feedback is always welcome at DanielJDonaldson.com.

-12-

Enjoying Covenant Communion

✠

*What if the communion ceremony is to be
more like a wedding than a memorial service?*

Over the centuries, several words have come into use to describe
the short ceremony initiated for Christians by Jesus, wherein
bread and wine are consumed. It is called by some the Eucharist, others
the Lord's Supper, or the Lord's Table. Most would know what ceremony you speak of when calling it Communion.

All Christians should acknowledge our eternal salvation was accomplished by the actual sacrifice of the physical body and blood of Jesus
on the cross. To put His sacrifice in the correct context, Jesus told us for
the joy that it brought to Him, He gladly did it.[47] His sacrifice was more
than a payment for the debt of the sin of humanity. Jesus invited us to
take part in a covenant-making ceremony to celebrate the new relationship this sacrifice would make possible, the New and Better Covenant.

Jesus is welcoming us to participate in the *joyful* remembrance of the
night of our blood-covenant redemption. For many, this fact is lost to a

---

47 Hebrews 12:2

tradition of couching the observance in the somber funeral-like tones of a memorial service.

What if the communion ceremony is to be more like a wedding celebration than a memorial service? Jesus wanted us to not just remember His death, He wanted us to remember the New Covenant which the sacrifice of His blood and body ratified. How can we at the same time reverence and recognize the blood and body of Jesus at communion, while sharing His joy and love in our remembrance of it?

To understand and enjoy Communion to a greater degree than ever before, we must look at the origins of the covenant-ceremony remembrance Jesus presided over called the Passover Meal. For hundreds of years, the ceremony was virtually unchanged. During this last Passover observance, its hidden truth was revealed and its meaning transformed with the handful of words Jesus added to their ceremony, to make it His own.

The Children of Abraham's Covenant Ceremony

On the night of their deliverance when death stalked all of Egypt, God preserved and protected His children and renewed their awareness of being a covenant people. After decades of slavery, the Hebrew children became unaware of their covenant rights and relationship. Their mindset makeover, changing from slaves to a covenant people, did not change overnight, but it started that night.

Moses was given very specific directions by God on how the people were to conduct a covenant-making ceremony. This ceremony reaffirmed for them the covenant promises made to their ancestor Abraham. Specifically, the type of ceremony performed is known as a *threshold* blood-covenant ceremony. Key portions of the ceremony emphasize how the covenant makers are not just becoming partners in a mutually beneficial covenant agreement, they are becoming family. This was discussed in detail in the prior chapter of this book that reveals the mystery of the Threshold Blood Covenant.

After leaving Egypt, God did not want His people to forget their covenant again. He instituted an annual set of feasts, festivals, sacrifices, and other remembrances. Some communal feasts were more significant than others. All of them had physical ceremonial practices that helped to bring spiritual and historical truths to their remembrance. Scholars make a strong case for how the symbolic elements of tabernacles, light, water, bread, wine, animal sacrifices, and more in these observances teach about the old covenants and at the same time foretell of the coming of the Messiah, Jesus.

The most sacred feast and ceremony on the Hebrew calendar was designed to remind Israel of the night they ate a covenant meal, sprinkled blood on their doorposts, and were delivered out of Egypt. This is the meal that is called the Seder or Passover Meal. Annually, on the designated evening, they celebrate and bring to remembrance the night their ancestors took part in a threshold blood-covenant ceremony, whereby they became aware again of their covenant with God.

For hundreds of years, even to this day, this event helps Israel remember the night of their deliverance. The angelic messenger of God's wrath did not enter homes having the marks of the blood covenant on their doorways and God lead His people out of Egypt. The Passover Meals have the look and feel of a small family wedding in the home. There is a normal festive meal, special table settings, and a plate of symbolic ceremonial food and drink. There are songs, dancing, and stories. Even though they will be remembering slavery, bondage, the death of a sacrificial lamb, and sorrows along the way, it is a joyous celebration of God's love, deliverance, provision, and the coming of the Redeemer.

The children take part in the festivities. They ask four well-rehearsed questions as part of the ceremony. The children play a symbolic hide and seek game with a piece of matzo bread. Three pieces of ceremonial matzo, apart from what is eaten during the meal, are wrapped in linen and placed one upon another. At one point in the ceremony, the middle piece is removed from the stack and a prayer of thanks for the bread is spoken over it. Next, the bread is broken and wrapped again in the linen. It is then hidden in the room while the children close their eyes. After the game, the child who found the prize returns it to the head of the household officiating at the head table. The leader barters a bit, then pays the child a ransom in coins to buy back the bread. It was assumed that these three pieces of bread represented Abraham, Isaac, and Jacob. A Jewish man who became a Messianic Christian told me, "I always wondered why we broke poor Isaac."

All of the observances pointed back in time and forward in time. They remembered a time of deliverance from Egypt and they also looked forward to the Messiah, who would deliver them again and bring God's presence back to every home. Four symbolic cups of wine are used at different points in the ceremony to celebrate God's deliverance. A seat was left unoccupied, waiting for the prophet Elijah who one day would precede and announce the coming Messiah.

More than anything else they did, the Passover covenant meal cemented the relationship between the children of Israel and their God. Hundreds of years after their hearts departed and their disobedience silenced the prophets, after being removed from their land by pagan kings and returning to scorched earth, they still continued to observe the Passover. Even after seeing Rome, the greatest of all pagan world powers, conquer their land, Israel was still faithfully observing the Passover Meal when Jesus began His ministry.

Jesus' New and Better Covenant Ceremony

Throughout His life, Jesus participated in the week-long Feast of Unleavened Bread, culminating in the final celebration known as the Passover. Leaven can represent sin and an effort is made to remove leaven or sin from their homes and lives. During the Passover meal, unleavened bread, called matzo, plays an important role.

For more than twenty-five years, Jesus participated first as a child and then as the rabbi at the head table. Imagine knowing what Jesus knew and having to endure the ceremony that in so many ways was designed to reveal Him, yet not deviate one syllable from obscuring the traditional celebration. For many, its promises of a Messiah seemed hollow. They were crushed by heathen rule, silent prophets, and their own hypocritical spiritual leaders heaping burdensome laws upon them.

The traditional focus in Christendom on the night of His last Passover meal highlights the bickering of some disciples over ascendency and the sad betrayal of Jesus by Judas during the meal. Countless times, before partaking of the elements, I have been told to make sure I was not still harboring some sin in my heart. Then I was to remember how much pain and suffering our sin caused and how great the price paid. The bread and drink were to remind us the price for our sin was that the sinless Jesus was tortured and His body and blood sacrificed on a Roman cross to pay for our sins. The mood is somber, with head bowed.

What was the ceremony Jesus performed like? Did He dwell on the sinfulness of the disciples? It certainly was present, but it was not the focus of what Jesus said when He began to recite the ceremony of old.

Jesus chose to give us a way to remember our covenant during a ceremony that was a celebration, not a funeral. Passover celebrated four outcomes of the covenant meal being remembered. These four outcomes were being freed from slavery, being taken out of Egypt, being redeemed by the arm of God, and the joy of fellowship as His family. Each segment culminated in a toast, drinking from one of the four cups of wine set forth to use for this purpose.

For Jesus, this evening's meal was a most glorious event that fulfilled a lifelong heart's desire.

> *Then He said to them, "With fervent desire I have desired to eat this Passover with you **before** I suffer."* (Luke 22:15 NKJV emphasis added)

Why did He joyfully look forward to this Passover with fervent desire? It is the time and place that Jesus would, at last, be allowed to retire the observance of the old covenant, reveal Himself as the promised redeemer, and usher in the new and better covenant. There was a celebration as always, including food, singing, and fellowship. Their bickering did not bother Him; Jesus used it as a teaching moment. The betrayal did not surprise or dismay Him; it was required for the rest of the evening to unfold as needed. Jesus just told Judas to go do it quickly.

It was now, at last, time for Jesus to implement the new covenant while fulfilling the old one. They came to the place in the observance when three pieces of ceremonial matzo, apart from what is eaten during the meal, are wrapped in linen and placed one upon another. Jesus takes out the middle piece, but does not hide or symbolically bury it. Instead, He reveals what had previously been hidden.

> *Now as they were eating, Jesus took bread and, praising God, gave thanks and asked Him to bless it to their use, and when He had broken it, He gave it to the disciples and said,* **Take, eat; this is My body.** *(Matthew 26:26 AMPC emphasis added)*

Before we delve into the verse above, let's recall earlier in His ministry when Jesus said and did something very similar, prefiguring, foreshadowing this event. We see truths in scripture more than once when they are important, as two witnesses are important in substantiating truth. First, the Old Testament, Father God demonstrates love for His people by providing an inexhaustible daily supply of bread in the Wilderness with a bread-like substance called manna. Next, Jesus demonstrates during His years of ministry that He is the Manna, the true, real, supernatural version of bread from heaven. Jesus does this by feeding more than five thousand people with a few loaves of bread. Jesus lifts the bread to the Father God, gives thanks for it, and prays that God blesses it to their use. Then Jesus hands it out to His disciples.[48] As He does, it is blessed, multiplied, increased from a small amount to an

---

[48] Matthew 14:19-21

amount that would feed all that were present in a way that can only be described as supernatural. In the multiple instances of these meals, the inexhaustible supply of Jesus, the Manna, is added to the physical bread in a way that increases it to their use. In the end, there was no less of Him, but more of the bread by what He mysteriously, supernaturally added to it from Himself and handed to others to partake of.

Fast forward now to the Passover night. Jesus reveals that the three pieces of matzo in the stack actually represent three persons of the one Triune God—Father, Son, and Holy Spirit. In any covenant meal, not just this one, the bread always represents the bodies of the covenant makers. The bread wrapped in linen and buried represents, in the old covenant ceremony, the body of Jesus which would also be wrapped in linen and buried. It has no leaven (sin) in it. The matzo is pierced and has scorch marks on it from the cooking process in a pattern of stripes and bruises. It never could have represented anything but the body of Jesus. Now Jesus reveals that it is His covenant-bread body.

It is the same Father-Son prayer as was spoken on the hillsides when feeding the masses which precedes handing out this bread during this sacred and vital part of the new blood-covenant ceremony. Jesus gave thanks, asked God to bless it, broke the bread, and gave it to His disciples. They received the bread and what was mysteriously, supernaturally imparted to the bread by Jesus, as He declared, "Take eat, this is My body." As they accepted and ate it, the bread became the covenant meal token of the sacrifice of His body and sealed the covenant to their great benefit. They, in turn, would repeat the ceremony, giving the bread of life to their disciples, and so on. The blessing is imparted, not to mere thousands for just a day, rather to us and untold millions for eternity.

By eating covenant-meal bread, you are agreeing to give your bodies, each for the other. In the wedding ceremony, jubilant, yet sacred and holy, the bodies are happily, not forcibly, not treacherously, but freely and fully of their own will, with joy, given to and for one another, till death do they part.

As we have seen, there are four cups of wine at Passover representing a progression of covenant promises in Exodus 6:6-7. The third cup is taken immediately after the meal. It is this cup representing the promise to redeem the partakers which Jesus takes as His own. It is called in the observance of Passover the Cup of Redemption, or of the Cup of the Redeemer. Exodus tells us that God promises, with an outstretched arm,[49] to redeem His people. Jesus lifts this cup to God, giving thanks and asking God to bless it to their use. Now, Jesus rewrites the old blood covenant ceremony to be bringing to our remembrance, as oft as we do it, the blood of the New and Better Covenant and His outstretched arms on the cross.

> *And He took a cup, and when He had given thanks, He gave it to them, saying, Drink of it, all of you;* **For this is My blood of the new covenant,** *which [ratifies the agreement and] is being poured out for many for the forgiveness of sins.* (Matthew 26:26-28 AMPC emphasis added.)

As we have seen take place in the blood-covenant ceremonies of old, it is very common in making a blood covenant for just a few drops of the blood of the covenant makers to be added to the wine. In this way, when the cup was shared saying, "This is my blood," the cup held both literally and figuratively the blood of the covenanters. They added a physical presence of their blood to the physical wine.

When Jesus asks Father God to receive thanks and bless it to our use, the same thing which no doubt makes the bread more than just bread, makes the wine more than just wine. Jesus adds supernaturally, mysteriously, the supernatural presence of the blood of the covenant maker to the wine. This impartation is more real than the addition of physical

---

[49] Exodus 6:6 Note: the reference to the outstretched arm is an amazing example of both covenants being represented. Father God stretched out His arm with powerful acts of judgment to win Egypt's release, and Jesus redeeming us with His arms outstretched on the cross.

blood, it is supernatural. This covenant is not just limited to temporarily impacting the physical flesh and blood of mankind for a lifetime. This is a supernatural and eternal covenant, consecrated by the supernatural and eternal substance of Jesus; imparting eternal life to the reborn spirit of men and women who eat and drink of it.

The reason that only His blood and body are added to the covenant elements is because only the shedding of His blood is required to ratify the new and better covenant. This is the chief reason it is a better covenant. The blood of Jesus covers for us, ours is not required. When they accepted the wine representing His blood-covenant sacrifice, they were committing to and accepting the blood covenant it represents.

We have seen how at a wedding ceremony there is a specific moment when the couple partakes of covenant cake and wine. In marriage ceremonies in Galilee at the time of Jesus' ministry, the groom offered the cup to the bride. Once she accepted his blood-covenant cup, they were now betrothed and covenanted together.[50]

It is not only in terms of the joyous tone of the ceremony that makes communion like a wedding ceremony. In another mystery, Jesus is taking the partakers who collectively make up the Church to be His bride.

As the covenant-wedding ceremony concludes, it is all blessings, promises, love, food, and fellowship. The two separate families have become one. Covenant makers and their now enlarged family will have a more intimate relationship than ever before.

✠

Immediately after supper, Jesus begins speaking and acting as if His sacrifice already took place, as if all the benefits of a blood-covenant relationship are now being given to the disciples.

✠

---

[50] Marriage Practices in Galilee–Documentary Film *"Before the Wrath"* by Kevin Sorbo. 04/16/20 www.ExplorationFilms.com.

We notice after the Passover ceremony is concluded, this same new intimacy like what would be in marriage is present like never before. It is intimacy not only with Jesus, but also with (Covenant Maker) Father God. Jesus speaks in an entirely new way to the disciples. Why? How can this be? Jesus has not yet died or been raised from the dead.

✠

Once the New Covenant ceremony was completed, the blood and body of Jesus were now pledged with an unalterable blood-covenant oath, to be given to His covenant-meal recipients.

✠

Having accepted His blood and body sacrifice during that ceremony, the disciples were now in a blood covenant. They had accepted Jesus as Lord and His promised covenant sacrifice was now as sure for them as the Word that upholds heaven and earth.

The disciples were very surprised that Jesus was no longer speaking in parables and veiled truths. Jesus was free now to reveal and share intimate truths of His relationship with the Father, His new relationship with His disciples, and their new relationship with the Father. It is here that Jesus explains how before this they always asked Jesus for everything, but now they will ask the Father and Jesus will add His prayer to theirs on their behalf. The new relationship is not only limited to those present at the covenant-making ceremony that just concluded, but to all who accept the word of these covenant witnesses and the blood covenant.

> *"I do not pray for these alone, but also for those who will believe in Me through their word; that they all may be one, as You, Father, are in Me, and I in You; that they also may be one in Us."* (Jesus in John 17, 20-21)

Taking Communion

Moses gave specific instructions for the initial covenant ceremony in Egypt, and then a way to keep reminding them of their covenant every year with the Passover Meal. Jesus introduced the New Blood Covenant at the Last Supper, the last Passover Meal that as Messiah He presided over. The Old Covenant was now done away with. Jesus was the final sacrifice of blood required to fulfill, complete, and set aside the law, and the other trappings of the old covenant festivals, sacrifices, dietary laws, ceremonial cleansing, and other annual rituals.

Just as for Israel, it was the intent of Father God, Jesus, and the Holy Spirit to bring the New Covenant to our remembrance on a regular basis. We must remain covenant aware. This short and sweet ceremony is meant to be the way to do it. If we are to be enjoying our covenant grace, covenant faith, and covenant favor, we must remember our blood-covenant relationship with the Father, Son, and Holy Spirit.

✠

**The ceremony Jesus first conducted,
and then told us to continue to do on a regular basis,
is celebrating His offering and our accepting the New Blood
Covenant. It reminds us of what was accomplished for us
by this grace-based covenant's sacrifice Lamb, Jesus Christ.**

✠

Being covenant aware is the whole point of taking what we call Communion. Communion was not intended to be avoided because of a guilty conscience or to make us feel guilt and sorrow because of our sins. It is to make us rejoice as it reminds us that our sins are already and completely forgiven.

Often protestant observances of Communion add in a passage Paul wrote to the Corinthians, a passage only meant for correction.

This passage is not included in other places where Paul speaks of the Communion ceremony.

It is implied by some that we might make the mistake of partaking in an unworthy manner by not repenting of recent sin just before partaking of the elements. If just temporarily refraining from some sin would make us worthy, I believe we would not have needed a savior to make us worthy by shedding His blood. We need to live perpetually thankful that all of our sins are forgiven, and mindful that it is His grace that has made us worthy to partake of and celebrate Communion. The believer should approach the Communion Cup the same way we do the Throne of God, without any condemnation, recognizing our perfection is not what brought us here, but rather His.

Paul said that in their observance, the problem was that they were not discerning the Lord's body.[51] If they were to come to their senses and discern the Lord's body, they would have ceased their unchristian behavior, finding health for their bodies and forgiveness of their sins.

The Apostle Paul, who wrote two-thirds of the New Testament, told us more about the grace-based blood covenant than any other biblical writer. Paul quoted Jesus saying, "This cup is the **new covenant** in my blood." Paul explains to the Corinthians who were behaving poorly at the communion feasts, how their behavior reveals that they are not covenant aware. They are undiscerning of the body of Jesus providing the covenant promises of health and healing for their flesh. He goes on to explain how this is why they were sick and dying young. They had lost sight of the covenant promise that by His stripes we are healed. We do not need to sin openly or secretly to lose sight of the blood-covenant promises. You may never have been told that the Communion ceremony is a blood-covenant ceremony and what that can mean to your life.

Communion is our covenant-ceremony meal. It is to remind us of the benefits and blessings that come to us by virtue of our grace-based blood covenant. The bread of communion is taken into us. In this way,

---

[51] 1 Corinthians 11:29

the covenant body of Jesus is taken into us; covenant-promised health and provision for the body are taken into us. The cup of communion is taken into us. In this way the covenant blood of Jesus is taken into us; covenant-promised eternal life is taken into us.

Enjoying Covenant Communion

There is no reason to avoid taking Communion with others, even if some of the text used in their observance leaves the partakers still unaware of its covenant significance. There is a benefit to participating with a local body of believers in prayer, praise, baptisms, and communion.

The admonition in scripture to remember our covenant was changed from the old covenant observance once a year, to now be as often as you choose to do it. There is no arbitrary limit to frequency or location. The observance need not be limited to a corporate setting. We can benefit from acting as the priests of our homes in our homes.

> *"And [Jesus Christ] hath made us kings and priests unto God and his Father."* (Revelation 1:6 KJV)

I encourage you to take Communion in a way that will allow you to enjoy it as intended, as a celebration and remembrance of our grace-based covenant with Jesus. Here is an example of scriptural text helping make us more aware of this being our covenant meal when we take Communion. You are free by grace to express your love and thanks for our blood covenant in any way you choose, as oft as you do it.

> *Thank You, Lord, for reminding us that while it is good to take stock of where we are in our daily walk, it is our being in You that cleanses us even now of every sin and qualifies us to receive the benefits of Your grace by faith. We love You and thank You for cleansing us of all unrighteousness and inviting us to now partake of Communion with You.*

Our Father in Heaven, we thank You for Jesus, Who has bid us come to partake of our New Covenant meal. We thank You for and ask You to place Your blessing upon the bread. Jesus, we proclaim and discern that the bread we now receive is Your body, given for us. We take it, break it, and eat together. We rejoice that by Your covenant body being pierced and broken, our bodies are made in every way whole. We receive the healing provided for our flesh now, in the Name of Jesus.

Father, we now thank You for and ask You to place Your blessing upon the Cup of the New Covenant, the Cup of Blessing. Jesus, we proclaim and discern that this drink is Your blood, shed for us. We take it and drink it together. We rejoice that by Your blood being poured out, our spirit man drinks in all of its benefits. We are redeemed, fully forgiven of sin, made righteous, and in every way that pertains to life and godliness, made whole in the name of Jesus.

Key Points: Review and Reflect

What if the communion ceremony is to be more like a wedding than a memorial service? What would be different?

What element of the old blood-covenant ceremony called the Passover Meal was revealed to be representing the covenant body of Jesus?

Which cup of the old blood-covenant ceremony was revealed to be the one representing the covenant blood of Jesus?

Continue to record in your journal how the impact of what you are learning is affecting your life.

Your feedback is always welcome at www.DanielJDonaldson.com

*About forty years ago, my young family and I had the fortune to live near the *Church on the Way* in Van Nuys, California. Long before megachurches were cool, and for the first time in my life, we had to wait outside of the church on the steps until the prior service attendees cleared out of each overflowing service. If you were not there early, you might not get a seat in the sanctuary. The pastor was the well-known writer of hundreds of worship songs still used to this day in many church services, Dr. Jack Hayford. This church would grow to acquire and use blocks of real estate along Sherman Way for their church and college. Communion at this church was a natural flow from awesome worship, to the observance of communion as part of that celebration. I never forgot the words Pastor Jack used to reset the observance to the correct tone. He said this is not about you or what you did, it is about Jesus and what He did. "You cannot take the cup and drink from it, with your head bowed. You must hold your head up, just as we do when we praise and worship Jesus."

A Final Word: Wineskins

As you begin to step out in faith and enjoy Covenant Grace, Covenant Faith, and Covenant Favor, you may hear voices telling you how important it is to balance the message of grace and faith, with keeping the law and with an awareness of the sins in your life. The pastor might kick off a ten-week series on how important it is to try to keep the Ten Commandments. A voice might seem to come from inside your own head saying, "You have to focus on your sin, deal with it, and fight it. You have to do good works and work at your salvation. You need to be praying and fasting more often. After all, don't you care about pleasing Jesus?"

> No one puts a patch from a new garment on an old garment; if he does, he will both tear the new one, and the patch from the new [one] will not match the old [garment]. And no one pours new wine into old wineskins; if he does, the fresh wine will burst the skins and it will be spilled and the skins will be ruined (destroyed). But new wine must be put into fresh wineskins. And no one after drinking old wine immediately desires new wine, for he says, the old is good or better. (Luke 5:36-39)

The Siren call to serve the Law is not a new problem. It began before Jesus even went to the cross. Jesus said John the Baptist was the greatest teacher, preacher, prophet, and priest of the Old Covenant. It was part of John's mission to exhibit adherence to the letter of the Covenant of Law. John's disciples were required to keep to a very strict code of conduct and more than once it really bothered them. John's followers had to keep strict dietary, Sabbath, ceremonial washing, and other laws. They were to have no contact with unclean people, places, or things. Jesus, quite to the contrary, ignores Sabbath taboos and hand-cleaning rituals, eats with known sinners, and accepts despicable tax collectors as friends. They see that the disciples of Jesus, the teacher their teacher looks up to, *do not even fast!*

In response to their criticizing Him for not making His disciples fast, Jesus, as was so often the case, answered with a parable. The critics of Jesus and His disciples were trying to force the new grace-based covenant-relationship wine into the withered, dry, and rotting Old Covenant Law wineskin.

The greatest difficulty, the most frustrating battle that the Apostle Paul had to constantly deal with, was criticism from people with an old Law and a sin-consciousness mindset. Paul's enemies were using some of the same "you are not acting righteous enough" tactics to shove the new grace-based covenant wine into the old law-based covenant wineskin. The freedom the new wine provided offended their sensibilities. As Jesus went on to say, His detractors had acquired a taste for others revering their show of holiness, devotion, good works, and law-keeping. They liked the old wine.

Paul warned the Galatians to beware of the Judaizers. These were the Jewish believers who were okay with letting the Gentiles receive Jesus as Lord, as long as they would become circumcised like Jews, keep the Sabbath of the Jews, honor their dietary laws, and make the new fledgling Church of Christ in essence, a small sect of Judaism.

Wanting to make all new converts fall in line under them, pious Jewish religious leaders traveled to Galatia. They sought to impose upon the Galatian Gentiles, who Paul had won over to the Gospel, the need to also follow the old covenant laws in order to obtain complete righteousness with God. Paul countered their condemnation of freedom from the demands of the Law with the truth.

> *Now it is evident that no person is justified (declared righteous and brought into right standing with God) through the Law, for the Scripture says, The man in right standing with God [the just, the righteous] shall live by and out of faith and he who through and by faith is declared righteous and in right standing with God shall live. Christ purchased our freedom [redeeming us] from the curse (doom) of the Law [and its condemnation] by [Himself] becoming a curse for us, for it is written [in the Scriptures], Cursed is everyone who hangs on a tree (is crucified); To the end that through [their receiving] Christ Jesus, the blessing [promised] to Abraham might come upon the Gentiles, so that we through faith might [all] receive [the realization of] the promise of the [Holy] Spirit.* (Galatians 3:11, 13-14 AMPC)

It is love that compelled God to redeem us, freeing us from not only the penalty of sin when we die, but from being constantly condemned by it while we yet live. God loved Abraham and His descendants, those who come from inside and outside the old blood covenant. Love prompted Father God to make the New Covenant cut, sign, and sacrifice, be nothing less than the body and blood of Jesus.

Out of God's inexhaustible source of *hessed*, loving-kindness and tender mercy, the new covenant is crafted to be obtained by grace, which He also supplies. It is not obtained or maintained by keeping the Law.

Yet, the freedom residing in love and grace can be threatening to those who are accustomed to equating keeping the letter of the Law, with pleasing God. We all know we cannot now nor have we ever kept the Law perfectly. Yet, we may be tempted to add trying to do it back into the salvation that Jesus gave us, to pay Him back for His free gift.

It is, I believe, only demystifying and revealing the nature of blood covenants which can free Christians from continuing to be bound by sin and sin consciousness. Being aware of our blood-covenant relationship with God is the only way to have perfect righteousness that is not an imperfect byproduct of our own imperfect works.

✠

Just think what you can accomplish if you focus your life on already having right standing with God which Jesus gave you, instead of the indebtedness to sin that Jesus removed from you.

✠

Remember how hard John the Baptist and his followers worked to keep the laws of the Old Testament? Jesus told us about how none was greater than John at serving and pleasing God under the constraints of the Mosaic Covenant. He then went on to say, "Notwithstanding, he that is least in the kingdom (New Covenant), the unschooled novice believer in covenant with Christ, is greater than John." We now have something greater than our own goodness, scholarship, works, abstinence, or will power, to makes us perfectly righteous. We can fill our faith tanks with the trustworthiness of the God who never breaks His covenant word. God swore a covenant oath to our being accepted and made righteous the moment we choose Jesus to be our Covenant Lord. Our challenge now is to live like we believe this. When we do, our circumcised heart will give us visible godliness our head and flesh could never team up to achieve. Righteous living is not accomplished by what is pinned to our skin, but by what grows as fruit from within.

Will you choose to break free from any sin consciousness, any old wineskin traditions which would deny you the blessings and freedom of grace? If you ask the Father to help you do this, He will. Knowing and trusting God as our Covenant Father empowers us to live the Blood Covenant faith, grace, and favor kind of life.

This is the Covenant Faith, Grace, and Favor kind of life:

Walking in His grace, we are more conscious of the righteousness Jesus provided than of the sin it eradicated. We now have His righteousness, peace, joy, love, praise, glory, and grace. No longer hounded by unworthiness or condemnation, we are now prompted by love and empowered by grace to gladly do what Jesus asks us and equips us by grace to do for Him. We are extending the borders of His Kingdom. The result is to unleash God's great blessings of covenant grace, faith, and favor into our lives. We are blessed; happy, enviably fortunate, and spiritually prosperous—possessing the happiness produced by the experience of God's favor and especially conditioned by the revelation of His grace.

About the Author

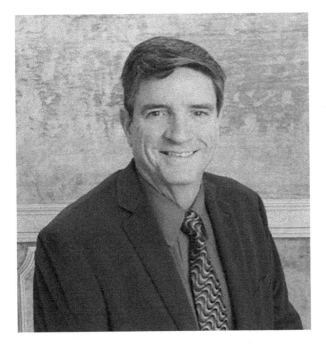

D aniel is a California native who grew up in the Los Angeles area and graduated from Westmont College, Santa Barbara. He earned a Bachelor of Arts Degree, magna cum laude, in English Literature with a minor in Biblical Studies. His senior year included a semester-long Bible Study Tour with his fellow student and new bride, Lindy, in Israel and Europe.

Daniel has always been active in teaching Bible studies and serving in other lay leadership roles in local churches, but had to balance that with a career to support his family. Participating in his father's electronics business from age twelve lead to Daniel's career in the fledgling microcomputer business. He opened and managed several of the first retail computer stores in Los Angeles.

Later in his technology career, Daniel became an early innovator of Digital Imaging products. Daniel's Micrographic Imaging solutions now provide digital access to microfilm collections at the US Library of Congress, research libraries, and other businesses worldwide. Business pursuits and life-long passions have taken Daniel to forty-nine US States and more than twenty other countries, racking up more than a million miles in the air.

In 2020, Daniel retired so that he could leverage a lifetime of biblical study, teaching, and practical application to enjoy entering full-time ministry. He lives in South Carolina with his wife of forty-eight years, Lindy, children Matthew and Sarah, and two grandchildren, Samantha and Kevin. Daniel is an author, Bible teacher, and public speaker. Contact Daniel or learn more at: https://danieljdonaldson.com/